Forward
and Away

Elisabeth Walker was born 1914 in
St Ives, Cambridgeshire. She trained as
a radiographer in 1935 and worked in
London. In 1938 she and her husband,
Dick, started training as teachers of
the Alexander Technique with F. M.
Alexander. They travelled extensively,
loving the outdoor life, especially
camping and mountaineering. They
lived in South Africa 1947–60 where
they taught the Alexander Technique
and raised their five children. After
their return to England they eventually
settled in Oxford where they ran a
teachers training course from 1985
to 2000. Through her many years of
teaching Elisabeth gave workshop
and master classes to teachers of the
Alexander Technique in Europe, USA,
Australia, New Zealand and Japan. Her
memoirs were first published in 2008.
Elisabeth continued to teach to within
a few weeks of death in 2013.

Forward and Away

Memoirs

Elisabeth Walker

Mouritz

First published 2008 by Gavin R. Walker.
This edition first published October 2014 by

Mouritz
6 Ravenslea Road
London SW12 8SB
United Kingdom

ISBN 978-0-9568498-4-7 Paperback

A CIP Catalogue record for this book
is available from the British Library

Layout and typesetting
by Jean M. O. Fischer

Set in Plantin in Adobe Indesign
Printed on 100gsm Opaque
by Imprint Digital, Devon, United Kingdom

Contents

Foreword

Jenny Holland

I first met Elisabeth Walker when I went to her for Alexander lessons in 1976. We were soon to become close friends, a friendship that has been a great delight for nearly thirty years. I went on to train as an Alexander teacher with Elisabeth and Dick and then to teach on her training course. Elisabeth's spirit is so extraordinary that it is hard to begin to describe the impact she has had on all who know her. I remember whilst I was training we had a visit from someone who was looking into ageing and wanted samples of Elisabeth's blood. Elisabeth was then into her 80s and working full time running the Oxford training course as well as taking her private pupils. We all thought it a joke, a contradiction in terms, to put Elisabeth's name in the same sentence as ageing. I can remember saying they would get a shock when her sample was examined and found to be full of sparkly and fizzy bits.

Elisabeth's story is a wonderful example of a life lived to the full, within the whole range of human experience. Her life has spanned nearly an entire century, and one that has seen enormous changes. One of her earliest memories is of a horse-drawn ambulance and she now finds herself at ease in a world of computers and cyberspace. She has an extraordinary ability to encompass and adapt to a very different world from the one she grew up in. Elisabeth has met adversity and pain with great courage and resourcefulness, and has welcomed joy and happiness with open arms. In her personal journey Elisabeth has acquired great wisdom and experience in her life as well as in her teaching. She is unique in now being the only first generation teacher, trained by Alexander himself, still living and working full time. As she has now been practising and teaching the Technique for over seventy years she is a perfect example of the benefits of the Technique and how we can use it to help us in our lives.

Elisabeth is a true adventuress, not only physically as in her trip across the Sahara, and moving to Africa with a young family, but also emotionally in her indomitable spirit and her whole approach to life. Being such a veteran traveller she has accumulated vast experience: she knows the nicest cafes and campsites as well as the best route across the desert and up the Matterhorn. The whole planet becomes her backyard.

Elisabeth's inexhaustible energy and enthusiasm runs through her life like a golden thread making her an exciting travelling companion, to say the least. In 1993 I went with her to Paris for the weekend to see the Matisse exhibition. Due to the popularity of the exhibition the tickets were timed, and when Elisabeth noticed ours had not been stamped she pointed out with great glee that we would be able go in again – which we did. It was a wonderful exhibition, but a very large one and after the second visit I was ready for a rest when to my amazement she said we ought to go to the Picasso museum as it was 'only round the corner and we ought not to miss an opportunity like that'. Our day concluded with a boat trip on the Seine, again something Elisabeth would not have contemplated missing. It promised to be a peaceful end to the day. Not so for Elisabeth as she ran round the boat taking pictures of Paris from every angle.

Elisabeth has the ability to give all of herself to those of us who are lucky enough to be part of her life: this as well as her wisdom and kindness make her a very special companion. Her delightful sense of humour and mischief never leaves her and she is as likely to dissolve in giggles now as when she was the young girl we learn of through her memoirs.

For several years these memoirs have been an ongoing project with which many people been involved at various stages. She has managed to complete them whilst also teaching her own pupils, teaching on training courses and travelling all over the world to take her master classes. Many were surprised when Elisabeth decided to publish the volume herself, having so far had no experience in this field. However she soon became au fait with publishing and printing terms, after getting on her bike and raiding the local library as well as scouring the internet and interviewing printers. She has now produced an enchanting story of her life and a glimpse of a lost world that is part of our history.

Jenny Holland

Introduction

Writing my life-story has brought back an intensity of emotions, both wonderful and tearful, that I found difficult to put into words. I wanted to include so much and to reflect the vividness of my experiences.

My photographs have prompted so many memories and printing them on my computer has brought me great pleasure. They have become my pictorial diary of friends and family, pupils and places wherever I have travelled.

I have been involved in FM Alexander's work (now known as the Alexander Technique) for seventy years and I am still learning. It is more difficult to be balanced and coordinated in one's nineties; aged bones, muscles, the whole functioning system slows down, one takes less exercise so it is even more essential to give thoughts to applying Alexander's principles.

Among the many important and special people in my life have been my parents, my husband Dick, my children, Alexander and his teaching. In recent years I have been teaching abroad so much and have now taught in fifteen different countries – meeting and learning from many other teachers. It has been a rich and rewarding time. It is the sum of these experiences that I have tried to set down here.

Elisabeth Walker
March 2008

The house in which Elisabeth was born

Elisabeth's aunts in party dress

1 Early Memories

I was born on a snowy night in December in 1914 as war was raging on several fronts in Europe and British ships were being sunk by German U-boats. In contrast the small, historic market town of St Ives on the banks of the Great Ouse in East Anglia was a haven of peace and tranquility.

St Ives is a picturesque market town dating from the tenth century. When I grew up there, it had a population of about 3,000 inhabitants. In the past, Samuel Pepys was a frequent visitor and Oliver Cromwell farmed and lived there; his statue stands in the market square. The prosperous cattle market thrived until 1946 when it closed. Since then many have discovered the attractions of St Ives and the population has increased five-fold. St Ives has one of only four medieval bridge chapels that still survive in England. As a child I was taught the verse that has always reminded me of home:

> *As I was going to St Ives*
> *I met a man with seven wives.*
> *Each wife had seven sacks,*

Each sack had seven cats,
Each cat had seven kits,
Kits, cats, sacks and wives,
How many were going to St Ives?

My paternal grandfather, Sir William Henry Clarke, a Quaker and a staunch Liberal, gained a knighthood for his work in that party in 1914. Years earlier, influential friends of his, the Cootes and the Warrens, who worked and lived in St Ives, invited my father to join their thriving firm of coal merchants. In 1907, when father married Lucy Cooke, a young woman from a nonconformist family in Gosport, her father built a house for them, overlooking the recreation ground, known to us as 'the rec'. In that house my brothers and I were born.

We enjoyed the freedom of meadows and river in this small community and knew most of the town's inhabitants. The house was so well situated. From the front gate we could turn left and walk directly into fields or turn right along a narrow path which led to an open tarred space in front of a row of primitive terraced houses. Occasionally, by mischance, we passed the night-cart collecting the sewage from these houses which had no WCs. We would spin our tops or bowl our hoops in this open space because there was no other traffic but cycles to impede.

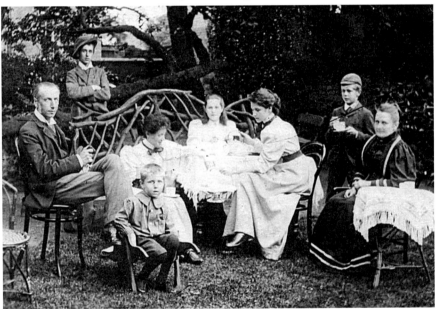

Clarke family, 1892

A family in this terrace had turned part of their front room into a small sweetshop selling gobstoppers, aniseed balls and ice-cream cornets. Often we spent our one penny weekly pocket money on a penny ice-cream cornet – the cream part was frozen Bird's custard. Gobstoppers were two for a penny; they were large and fun as we kept taking them out of our mouths to see them changing colour.

An early memory is of my father (who served in the Navy in spite of his non-combatant Quaker upbringing) coming home on leave in 1917 when I was two and a half. He was a good father but definitely head of the family and one to fear, so I learned to be careful to please him. That day I put too much saccharine in his tea; fortunately, he forgave me and took me into the garden to play with my two brothers Stuart, seven, and Philip, five and a half. As we grew older we had fun together in the garden, my elder brother showed me how to smoke Woodbine cigarettes in the empty chicken-house and at other times we built small fires and roasted potatoes in the embers. I enjoyed climbing trees with them. When Stuart's interest in ornithology required him to use climbing irons to reach heron's nests at the top of high trees I helped by putting rings on the featherless young as he roped them down to me in a bag. I disliked this task as the babies sicked up part digested eels as I held their bony frames. However, it gave me pleasure to help my big brother.

Elisabeth, aged 2, with father

Elisabeth, aged 2, with brothers Stuart and Philip

In March 1918 a horrific noise disturbed the family and local inhabitants when an aircraft from RAF Wyton crashed into the spire of the parish church. For the next six years scaffolding surrounded that spire and in the art class at school we were sent to sketch this many times.

In November 1918, a month before my fourth birthday, I was taken to our market hill beside the Cromwell statue to join the people celebrating the armistice. On the way there, I saw large posters of Lord Kitchener pointing to the passers-by saying, 'Your country needs you'. At the market place, I wondered why so many were crying – I didn't think grown-ups were allowed to cry. The crowds there were in contrast to later when the town streets were closed for the annual fair with its roundabouts, helter skelter (we called it 'penny-on-the-mat') and stalls selling their wares. This was a big event for several days and we children always looked forward to it.

It was in the 1920s that I first became interested in dress. My mother changed her style to the fashions of the time. Her former ankle-length skirts were shortened to the knee. Her waisted dresses became hand-knitted silk openwork tops, straight from shoulder to hip, totally shapeless, the neck and the cuffs decorated with rabbit's fur which I loved to touch. Her long locks of curly red hair, which she had worn in different shapes round her head, were cut off and styled in a bob. Suddenly she looked like a different person – I found the fashion severe with the bobbed hair and short shapeless garments. At that time, we three children were all dressed in sailor suits and sailor hats: mine had 'HMS Queen Elizabeth' on the ribbon, all very patriotic. I wasn't able to choose my clothing and I hated wearing leather gaiters to keep my legs warm, with lots of buttons up the side. I was very impatient as my mother dutifully did them up with her button-hook. Once there was a fancy dress party and I went dressed as a Quaker girl, in a grey ankle-length dress with white collar and white apron and a white cap, rather like a nurse's cap, very simple and demure. In contrast, my brother Philip went as the Mad Hatter, much more fun – and he won a prize. I rebelled against the pretty girl image and, later, a school friend and I went to a fancy dress party dressed as ruffians, meaning to resemble the 'Bisto' kids. As now, the makers of Bisto, a popular gravy substitute, used to depict on hoardings urchins wearing scruffy clothing being attracted to the aroma with the words, 'Ah, Bisto'.

Our musical education was nil, though we enjoyed listening to the gramophone with its large horn playing all the Gilbert and Sullivan operettas as well as one of my favourites, Ernest Lough singing 'O, for the wings of a dove'. Ever since, I have had a passion for the purity of the treble voice. I often go to the college chapels in Oxford and Cambridge to hear their choirs. Father loved Richard Tauber and Derek Oldham and other great voices of the period. In 1923, he built a crystal wireless set but it was not until 1926 when the BBC first broadcast that we could clearly hear broadcasts of news and music; this seemed like magic to us.

I have vivid memories of significant events. In 1923, we were taken to the British Empire Exhibition at Wembley. There were a number of fairground rides, like a ghost train and a watersplash ride, but I was too timid to go on these. I remember winning a doll at a hoopla stall. My brother said that it was favouritism but I thought it was skill. I remember the General Strike in 1926 when parents and friends and the grown-ups I knew all turned their hands to helping the country in different ways, like making cauldrons of soup and loaves of bread, while we children had to fend for ourselves. On 29 June 1927, we witnessed a total eclipse of the sun. I had to blacken glass pieces over a candle so that we could watch it without harming our eyes.

In our garden there were tool sheds, one providing a largish play space. There was also a tiny darkroom, and there, from the age of about ten, I developed and printed my own films. At that time one could print in the sun using daylight paper with the opportunity to check to see whether the print was dark enough. The result was sepia colour. I liked these and the

Above: Mother. Below: Elisabeth

simplicity of the processing. I have had a wide interest in photography ever since, developing and enlarging my own photos and recently embarking on digital photography. It was playing in that dark room as a child of ten that helped so much when I trained as a radiographer and had to do serious developing of films, often of the famous and wealthy.

I grew up with animals and have enjoyed their company as well as caring for them. Cats, dogs, hens have been part of my life. Ouser, my first cat, given that name because he was a good mouser, usually slept on my bed and brought his last catch, a mouse or part of a rabbit remains, to share with me. I did not like that at all. Nor did I like him teasing me by hiding and then jumping out to frighten me in the dark – he thought it was fun. I still loved to cuddle him. He came for walks in the 'rec', but when he heard the one o'clock buzzer sound from the local paper mill, he would run for our veranda door, which he could open: he knew it was his dinner time. My next cat was Smee. He was even more beautiful and more cuddly with a lovely grey coat but not as clever as Ouser.

I was not as close to our dogs. Tim, a wire-haired terrier, was a family dog, always with us but he especially loved my mother. The feeling was mutual for she cried a lot when he died. I liked the hens too, especially the broody ones when they sat on their eggs until the tiny fluffy chicks came out and we fed them on chopped hard-boiled eggs.

I had my own patch of garden, with a rockery and small space for lettuces and radishes on one side and pansies, marigolds and candytuft on the other. It gave me an interest in botany which became a favourite subject at school. Using my father's tools encouraged me to be practical. I think that those early days influenced the pleasure of using my hands in later life. Gardening has been one of my great joys and I have had good opportunities to create gardens in South Africa and in the Oxfordshire countryside.

My father's love of boating led to us being taught to swim and dive when quite young, and every morning from May to October he would take me before breakfast to dive into the river, often full of weeds and other unknown horrors. But to his 'Go on my girl!' there was no refusing. Father was always the boss but he was fair and determined that his children would not be overprotected or 'weedy', and I know that has helped me through life's difficult times.

The Great Ouse played a huge part in my early life. A friend living right on the river had otters as pets. The otters could swim in and out of an enclosure at the end of their garden, and when I went to tea my friend was wearing her favourite live one around her neck at the table. I was hor-

Elisabeth off to swim with her two brothers

Boating on the Great Ouse

Elisabeth aged 10 diving at the Frying Pan

rified later on when there was an otter hunt and men and dogs charged along the riverbank trying to catch otters. Many cruel activities seemed to be permissible.

We spent many hours punting, rowing, sailing, canoeing and swimming. I remember great consternation when in 1924 some 'monster' began overturning canoes and disturbing swimmers. It took some time for this creature to be caught – it was a giant sturgeon more than six feet

Elisabeth with friends on the river

Spare Moments arriving by lorry

Spare Moments

long. It was eventually displayed on a table in the Corn Exchange at St Ives and its roe was sent to King George V. We paid a penny to see this huge fish lying on a long table, no longer able to frighten us, although we were a little nervous of swimming in the river in case there were others still there. Fine weather brought many people on to the river in punts, rowing boats and canoes.

In the 1920s, my father brought a sailing boat in a lorry all the way from the Solent to the Great Ouse. The boat was called *Spare Moments*. We had some exciting sails aboard her. The happiest times were with three girlfriends, camping with a tent on our own. We were thirteen or fourteen years old and so free. The outboard motor on the stern was difficult to start. We cursed and swore as we vainly pulled the cord. At last, we started it and joyfully cruised along to Hemingford Church where we tied up and walked through the village lured by the smell of baking bread. There was a huge bake-oven and a friendly baker hooking out hot loaves with his 'spade'. The smell of newly-baked bread whetted our appetites and we would hurry back to eat it on board.

We cooked in the cabin on a primus stove which had the nasty habit of flaring up and singeing our hair so we soon learned caution, though one of my friends let a billy-can of Bird's custard boil over on the primus and it ran into the bilges. I remember being very cross at having to bail out custard. When it rained we put on swimsuits and fished. We caught bream, full of small bones, which we cooked to eat. I once caught an eel

Sketch of the Sturgeon by Tim Toomey

but could not take it off the hook as it was too slippery – it wiggled its way off eventually. Caught out once during a severe thunderstorm, we had the sense to anchor *Spare Moments* in the middle of the mill pool away from the tall trees. It was scary but exciting ... eventually, we heard calls from the bank – our parents had driven the three miles from home to see that we were safe.

We were encouraged in many outdoor activities, such as skating when the flooded meadows froze over, and cycling to school across the allotments. Cycling back after dark, I was once stopped by a policeman because I had not lit my oil lamp. He knew I was lying when I said it had blown out, as he felt the lamp which was cold. No prison this time. The lamps used were fuelled with oil or acetylene and often I was caught out as I had no matches with which to light my lamp. In those days matches were so necessary. I used to go to bed by candlelight. Often the candle blew out and, not liking the dark, I shouted loudly until someone brought me matches. Father usually kept some in his pocket to light his pipe. It was an exciting day when electricity came to St Ives and Father had it installed. At the touch of a switch there was light. Soon after, we had the luxury of a fridge and a vacuum cleaner. Today we have washing machines and dish washers and we must all have televisions and computers. Modern technology has advanced so fast during my lifetime.

Ladies Day at St Ives Golf Club

In about 1920, father and his friends founded the St Ives Golf Club which became an important social centre, with whole families joining. We were all encouraged to play and this was an advantage when I met and married an international golfer – more of that later. Sophie, from the local workhouse, was employed to make simple teas including Dundee cake. She became an institution. Twice a week, Sophie and our maid Elsie went together to the Broadway cinema to see the silent films. Sometimes I went with them. Mime and comedy artists like Charlie Chaplin and Buster Keaton, not to mention the cartoon, Felix the Cat, did not need sound to be entertaining. Our resident maid played an important role in our family. I spent a lot of time in the kitchen with my mother or with one of our maids so I enjoyed baking: making marmalade, jams and ice-cream with cream and fresh fruit. In those days, to make ice-cream, we had to buy ice from the fishmonger.

The St Ives taxi was a horse-drawn cab and it waited outside the station. Once, Mother hired it to take her and me to a Christmas party. Halfway up Houghton Hill, the horse objected, and tried to turn in the shafts to look in at us. Mother said, 'I want to get out and walk', but I cried, 'I can't walk in my party dress' – which was blue-green taffeta shot with gold and frilled to the ankles. The cab did get us to the party where we played 'Oranges and Lemons', 'Here we come gathering nuts in May', and 'French Chairs' – the conventional games of the time.

As there was no Quaker Meeting House in St Ives, every Sunday we went to the nonconformist church in the market square. Our pew was

St Ives horse-drawn taxi cab

behind a man who had smelly brilliantine on his hair which made me feel sick. This together with the very long sermons made me fidget and make a fuss. Immediately after church, all five of us drove to my paternal grandparents who lived twelve miles away in Chatteris. Sunday lunch was always roast beef, Yorkshire pudding, potatoes and cabbage. Pudding was often apple pie or Eccles cake. At lunch the conversation was of politics and important persons. One person mentioned a good deal was Lord Peckover. My grandfather always seemed to me to be going off to Peckover House. He was a banker and he advised Lord Peckover's daughter Alexandrina on her financial affairs. Later on I was to meet Lord Peckover's grandson Roland Penrose.

At Christmas, Grandpa always received a whole Stilton from the Peckovers. My parents used to be sent home with half of it and it would stink out our larder for weeks. Violet, who came to help on Mondays and Tuesdays with washing and ironing, and our maid Elsie enjoyed the strongly smelling Stilton with their mid-morning tea as it got riper and riper. We children would hold our noses whenever we went into the kitchen. A more pleasant smell came on washdays when the linens were boiling in the copper and the steam wafted through the kitchen. It was all very hard work because, after the steaming, the linen had to be rinsed in galvanized tubs, put through the hand mangle and hung in the garden. Whoever did the ironing took an iron off the kitchen range and spat on it to test its heat.

Elisabeth swimming with Betty

HRH Queen Elizabeth II visiting Betty at Benenden

My cousin and namesake Elizabeth Clarke, usually called Betty, being an only child, often stayed with my grandparents and I went too to keep her company. I was a few months older and also called Elisabeth Clarke, though my parents added Helen before it to please Granny. Betty and I had very little in common. She was an intellectual and could answer all grandfather's mealtime quizzes and made me feel very stupid and inferior. At the age of eight Betty would be reading *Strand* magazines while I was making lavender bags on Granny's treadle sewing machine. It was from that age I developed an interest in dressmaking. Later when I brought friends in from Chatteris to run sports on the croquet lawn, Betty was still devouring books. She later became a teacher and magistrate, then from 1954 to 1975, headmistress of Benenden School, where she taught Princess Anne. Betty's nickname there was 'Celeste', from the Babar books. Later, she was awarded the CVO for services to the Royal Family.

My mother's mother and three of her sisters all lived in Gosport and Alverstoke. Our visits to them and to Chatteris were always in Pa's latest

Chatteris: Back Row: Uncle Geoff, Aunt Winnie, Uncle Ken, Aunt Edie, Father - Clive
Middle Row: Aunt Dollie, Grandfather - Sir William, Brother - Stuart,
Grandmother - Lady Florence (Clarke), Mother - Lucy
Front Row: Elisabeth, Brother - Philip, Cousin Betty

Family Motorbike

The De Dion Bouton

vehicle. At one time it was a motorbike and sidecar with the five of us: mother, Philip and I in the sidecar, and Pa and Stuart on the bike. Then came the De Dion Bouton, the Rover and the Daimler. They were all two seater cars with a dicky (two seats in the back of the car under a lid) where we children sat. It was often cold and wet travelling until my father built what he called the rabbit hutch to cover the dicky and then we children were quite snug in there. In the summer holidays we drove to Gosport, travelling through Windsor Great Park at never more than thirty miles per hour. It took us a whole day.

Staying with my maternal grandmother was quite formal; she was an ardent nonconformist so we said prayers in the dining room before breakfast. We all had to be there, including the maids in their starched caps and aprons. Meals were announced by a large gong in the hall which sounded five minutes before each meal. A little black dog called Rikki Tikki Tavi (named after the mongoose in Rudyard Kipling's *The Jungle Book*) sang to the gong every time. Ivy Compton Burnett's novels always take me back to the atmosphere of Granny's strict regime.

On Sundays mornings we all had to go to church, the sermons were very long and boring. At her home, no card games were permitted but we were allowed to do a jigsaw of Daniel in the Lion's Den or play hymns on the pianola. There was no alcohol but Mumby's ginger ale was permitted.

Those first nights in Gosport were made memorable by the smell of the sea and the sound of the fog horns or the 'peep peep' of the ferries crossing the harbour. I slept in my aunt's study. She was Commissioner for the Girl Guides and had a drawer full of badges. I once took some of

Arriving at Gosport

these to my cousins to show that we were a secret society. When this was discovered I was made to feel very guilty, like a thief.

Portsmouth Harbour has always been special to me. In the 1930s Camper Nicholson designed and built beautiful boats, many of which we saw being launched into the harbour. We were allowed to go on board and see the cabins, the galleys and the chartroom, all sleekly finished and ready for their maiden voyage. My brother Stuart was often asked to crew on these occasions.

There was so much to do on our visits to Portsmouth. There were cousins to play with, the sea to swim in and boats of every sort and kind. It cost a penny on the ferry for us to cross the harbour from Gosport to Portsmouth. This we were often allowed to do on our own. At low tide when the mud was exposed people used to throw pennies for children to collect. I remember seeing them covered in mud but triumphant as they found one. Nelson's Victory was there for us to climb on board as it is for all the hundreds of tourists today.

My grandmother had a bathing box on the beach at Stokes Bay. Hanging on the pegs in that bathing box were voluminous red and white striped and frilled bathing dresses, no longer worn because the grown-ups had stopped swimming. It was a pebbled beach – but we loved it and spent hours in an icy sea saying it was boiling. We wore ill-fitting cotton swim-

Portsmouth Harbour - ferry which cost a penny on the right

Elisabeth with camera on the Solent

suits that hung cold and loose when out of the water. Our fingers and toes grew white with cold but we were loath to come out of the sea.

We sailed on the Solent during Cowes Regatta week when the *Royal Yacht Britannia* and a large fleet of naval destroyers and an aircraft carrier were anchored off Cowes. The J-class yachts, which we had seen being launched into Portsmouth Harbour, were racing at that time. Huge yachts they were, carrying so much sail that their wooden masts sometimes broke leaving a splintered jagged stump rising from the deck. We sailed among them all, and at the end of the week were enthralled by a glorious fireworks display. The battleships were all lit up with fairy lights – a spectacular sight. I was reminded of that when, in 2004, I saw on TV the celebrations of the sixtieth anniversary of VE Day.

Having scarlet fever when I was twelve was an unpleasant experience. My parents were on holiday and had boarded me out with two elderly spinsters in an old-fashioned house. They were kind but fussy. One day cycling back from school I stopped to buy lozenges for a painfully sore throat. On my return my elderly friends were concerned as I felt worse and worse and

asked to go to bed, refusing food. The doctor was called and diagnosed scarlet fever. At that time it was a notifiable illness.

The WC was downstairs and very dark and difficult to find and my room seemed miles away. It was not so good when suffering from diarrhoea and vomiting. Eventually my parents were called back and I was sent off to hospital by myself in a horse drawn ambulance. A six-mile journey via Houghton Hill posed a difficulty for the horse and ambulance as the horse did not have quite the power to climb the hill. At last by use of whip and brake the driver succeeded. I was dumped in a very bleak hospital with a mortuary on one side and a cemetery on the other. I had a high fever and a burst ear-drum and stayed there in isolation for nine weeks alone until one other girl joined me. The nursing care was abysmal.

At the other end of the hospital were the diphtheria patients. Nurses came to and fro, one complaining of her sore throat, and sure enough the next day she was confined in the diphtheria ward. During these nine weeks we had no visitors, not even to talk through a window, but maybe it toughened me up. Even to this day I believe my gut has not recovered from the laxative cascara pills and not being allowed to get out of bed. The nurses rarely heard our shouts for a bedpan. It was such a relief later when we were allowed to get out of bed and find our way to the lavatory.

—

My primary school was Slepe Hall; it is now quite a posh hotel in St Ives. I first went to dancing class there aged four but I refused to take part until I had seen the others perform. Returning the next time, I joined in with enthusiasm and have liked dancing ever since. At the age of five I started at the kindergarten. I was friendly with a boy called Pat McGee. We were to be the two babes in the wood in the school play but two days before the show I fell and broke my collar-bone. I refused to perform bandaged up so that was the end of stage work for me. Pat was a friend until he was eight and came to say goodbye wearing a top hat, a black suit, and a white Eton collar. I thought he was in fancy dress. He was off to be a chorister at King's College, Cambridge. My parents used to take me to hear the choir in that historic chapel. It is still a huge thrill for me to return there. Choristers still wear top hats and Eton suits and the choir continues to do justice to that magnificent chapel.

I was happy at school until, at the age of eight, I had to board for a term because my mother was ill. Although I made friends with another young boarder, we were treated like babies. Every morning we had to kiss the headmistress's whiskery face and were given left-over foods for breakfast. My mother made up for my misery by arriving before the end-of-term fancy dress party with a fairy costume for me – it even had wings. I had never been so spoilt.

My best friend was Joan Anderson. Her father was a farmer up at Houghton Hill. He would often fetch us in his horse and trap to the farm for tea and play. Joan and I both had pet rabbits: she was allowed to have a whole family of them but I had just one called Wilfred. I had to care for him, clean out his hutch, and give him food and water. I always had a fear that I might find him dead, and this took away all the pleasure of having him.

At school I enjoyed hockey and netball but best of all athletics and in my last term there I won the athletics cup when my mother, who was a friend of the headmistress, was presenting the prizes. I still looked forward to going to boarding school having been told by my brothers what fun it could be.

Forward and Away

When I was thirteen, my parents took me to look at Quaker schools in York and Darlington. At Polam Hall in Darlington my father was amazed to meet again Oswald Baynes who had taught him at Bootham School in York. Baynes had married Helen Baynes, the headmistress at Polam. I believe that, as well as my liking the place, this clinched the decision for me to go to Polam, and I have been everlastingly grateful. I was timid and shy when I started, not really enjoying my first term but knowing that it was where I wanted to be and that I was going to enjoy it. During that first term I secretly determined to contribute and have my name on one of the honours boards that hung over the platform in the dining room. Achieving that goal gave me a lot more confidence. I believe the wonderful atmosphere of love and tolerance at school was bestowed on us all by that remarkable person Helen Baynes. She gave us something really special both at school and for our future lives. I made wonderful friends at Polam which I think set the pattern for making good relationships in my life and my desire to work with people. Ma B and Pa B, as we called our headmistress and her husband, treated us as their daughters during our time with them at Polam, with great interest in the well-being of each individual.

During my first year, when the pond froze and we skated, some mornings we had to break the ice on our wash water – no running water, just ewer and basin – but on colder winter nights we had coal fires in our bedroom. What luxury. There was complete freedom of choice regarding place of worship on Sunday mornings. With my friends, we worshipped at

Helen Baynes

Polam – Elisabeth receiving the Star Gym Cup

various churches and I most of all enjoyed the hymn singing. In the evening in school, a Quaker Meeting with hymns was held. Ma B would read to us with such clarity of diction that we would all listen with interest. One such book was *Barlash of the Guard*. A suggestion box gave us choice with whom we shared rooms and where. The happiest arrangement I remember was when six of us shared a room at Elm House.

One night Ma B, who slept on the ground floor, rang her bell and was found sitting up in bed under an open umbrella. She said: 'Please attend to the tap upstairs.' One of the girls had let the bath upstairs overflow. Ma B really was an exceptional lady.

My first visit to Europe was when a French teacher took me and a friend to Paris to improve our French. We stayed with a French family who showed us all the important sights in that beautiful city. Since then I have returned there many times with my own children.

Thanks to that remarkable headmistress, teachers and wonderful friends, I left school a more confident teenager.

When I left boarding school in 1932, my parents wanted me to spend some time at home. I spent the next year inviting my old school friends to stay with us in St Ives and I also stayed with them in Tayport, Dundee and the Highlands. When my friends came to stay we played golf, and spent time sailing and swimming in the river as well as playing tennis. I also went to Foxlease in the New Forest where I trained to be a Girl Guide and Brownie leader in order to work with the Brownies in St Ives.

In the following year my Aunt Edie and two cousins, Charles and Ken Blake, and I went to Grenoble where we joined student parties and daily trips to ski in that area and from there Edie and I took the coach over the mountains to Cannes where we met my mother's uncle Spencer, who spent winters in Cannes and summers in Switzerland. Edie was such fun to be with as she was like a close friend although she was older than my father. In the First World War, she was a nurse in the Isle of Wight at Osborne House which had become a hospital for wounded soldiers. Immediately after the war, she became the first matron of the Gosport War Memorial Hospital. When Betty and I were staying in Gosport we used to climb on the roof of that hospital watching operations through the sky-light. Edie retired from the war memorial hospital to look after her sister Aunty Win who was ill. They both lived in Alverstoke near Gosport and Edie, although retired, worked during the Second World War in a munitions factory to help the cause. But later when Cousin Betty was ill with typhoid at Benenden School, she looked after her and became a much loved character at that school. All the girls called her 'auntie'.

During holidays from school I had taught myself to make simple dresses. My parents would buy me material but no holiday clothes – a good incentive. When I started making grander ball gowns they said I was gifted and should be apprenticed to become a Court dressmaker, so I

Ice hockey at Grenoble

Aunt Edie and patients at Osborne House during the First World War

went to a Madame Calista in Wigmore Street supposedly to train. Actually I was an unpaid seamstress. There were ten to fifteen paid ones and they made it clear I wasn't one of them. I believe that was the only time in my life I have been bored. It was ghastly. After six weeks I went home with flu and never returned to Madame Calista.

Scotland has always been a special place for me and my parents. Two of my best friends from school, Mabel and Betty, came from Dundee and Tayport and I spent holidays with them in the Highlands. When we left school, the three of us stayed at the Cruden Bay Hotel north of Aberdeen, with my parents who stayed there regularly. This hotel, which belonged to the LNER Railway, was situated on a hill overlooking two golf courses by the sea. During early July it offered a great service, six-course meals and clean laundry daily, all for the sum of £1 per head per day. I stayed there first in 1933. It was easy to make friends. There were many young people there, and we became especially close to the Winton family. Their son Stanley was up at Cambridge. He was a golf blue and played for the Cambridge University team that included Willie Whitelaw, Laddie Lucas and

*Outside Cruden Bay Hotel – Pa, Eleanor & Stanley Winton, Mabel (schoolfriend),
Mother, Elisabeth, Betty (schoolfriend)*

John Lyon. Stanley and I would go to plays and films together. We loved
dancing and went to several May Week balls. I stayed with him and his
family at the Lake of Monteith (the only lake as opposed to loch in Scotland), one of their favourite holiday spots. It was beautiful and secluded
and we could swim in the nude.

*Part of an old Postcard showing Cruden
Bay Hotel*

Stanley Winton with Elisabeth

The Wintons became close friends and in 1936 they took me to play golf at Muirfield near Edinburgh, then Golspie and Dornoch, and round the north and north-west of Scotland, being driven by Mr Winton's chauffeur. That was a great holiday. It was through them that I learned to play golf to a higher standard. Stanley Winton and his sister, Eleanor, often stayed with my parents at St Ives. Sadly, Stanley lost his life at sea in the last war and beautiful El had a bad stroke. I owe a lot to the Wintons and remember them with great fondness.

Every year the Cruden Bay Golf Club Challenge Trophy was held and one year I was invited to present the cup to Mr Colin Brown, a great privilege. Later, during the war, the RAF took over the hotel, after which it became dilapidated and too expensive to repair so it was demolished and small bungalows were built in the grounds. The golf course remains and is as wonderful as ever. It was on the golf course at Cruden Bay that, in 1937, I met the love of my life.

Elisabeth presenting the cup to Mr Colin Brown

Middlesex Hospital

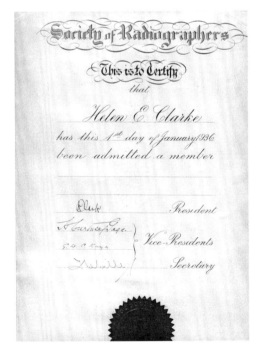

Elisabeth's certificate of membership of the Society of Radiographers

2 Forward

In 1934, I announced to my parents my wish to study medicine. It was discouraged as being too long and expensive to train and it was also comparatively unusual for a woman – I believe my father wanted me to stay at home. One day I happened to read about radiography and this excited me.

My mother was supportive so we trailed round London hospitals to find a place in a radiography school. I enrolled at the Middlesex Hospital which was just starting up a school. I started with three other students in January 1935. Because the school was not quite ready we worked in the basement. This was almost certainly illegal. The equipment in the basement was old. Uninsulated wires hung around the ceiling, sparks flew, and there was always a strong smell of ozone. It was a great day when the Duke and Duchess of York opened the new department on the ground floor. We had more dark room space and the films came along a conveyor direct from the patients' area to the darkroom.

The training regime was very concentrated. We studied anatomy, physiology, photography and advanced engineering. We learnt how to set up the radiograph machinery, position the patient and all the specific details of exposure times. In those days we did not take special precautions to protect ourselves against harmful radiation in the way that present radiographers do. We would develop, wash, print and fix. We were shown how to put radium needles into breasts to cure cancerous tumours. Our white caps and overalls were similar to those of the nursing staff. The atmosphere in hospitals was more disciplined and regimented than it is today and there was a clearly defined hierarchy in all departments.

There have been enormous developments in the field of radiography since I trained. At the Middlesex I studied both therapeutic and diagnostic work. Today, radiographers specialise in these fields and in other work: MRI, EMI, scanning, tomography and ultrasound, and radiographic treatment has become even more specific.

At the end of our training we had exams in each of the subjects. My oral exam was on my twenty-first birthday. The Consultant Radiologist at the Middlesex, Graham-Hodgson, said he had a job for the top student. I don't think I actually got top marks but I got the job, which was in Graham-Hodgson's private practice at 55 Upper Brook Street – now part of the American Embassy.

The leading physicians of the day, Lord Dawson of Penn and Sir Stanley Hewitt, sent many of their patients to our consulting rooms for diagnostic x-rays. Graham-Hodgson made his name taking x-rays of King George V. The king had respiratory problems and eventually died at 11:55am on 20 January 1936: I wrote it in my diary. It was later said that Lord Dawson gave him a lethal shot of morphine so that he should not continue to suffer. A week later the King's funeral took place in London and I joined the crowds in the streets. It was impossible to breathe with people pushing in all directions so I vowed I would avoid crowds in the future.

A radiographer colleague and I would sometimes make house visits. We went with our mobile apparatus to Marlborough House to x-ray Queen Mary. In London at that time there were varieties of electric currents: direct as well as alternating. When taking the portable to different houses we had to make adjustments to fit the existing electricity supply and there was always the risk that nothing would work. At that time, we had difficulty with the machine and to get it to work I had to put a hairpin in the fuse box. Queen Mary behaved in a regal way although she had an arthritic hip – there were no hip replacement procedures in those days. She would smile graciously as we made our bobs. Her bedroom was dark, hung with plum red drapery, with footmen hovering around.

As well as Queen Mary, other members of the Royal Family required x-rays. The then Duchess of York, who became Queen Elizabeth and then the Queen Mother, was delightfully friendly. 'How did you come to be here?' she would ask. Whenever royalty came to our consulting rooms, the hall would be filled with flowers. On one occasion, the Duchess of York, obviously charmed by our floral arrangement, said with a smile, 'The flowers are delicious.'

She was quite different from Wallis Simpson to whom I took an instant dislike, as she appeared arrogant and strained. This was before King Edward VIII abdicated to be able to marry her. I believe it was her anxious state, brought on by the indecision surrounding her relationship with Edward, that made all her radiographic examinations necessary. Day after day she would come. Graham-Hodgson spent ages with her, often working overtime. When I prepared her for x-ray, she would not wear our cotton gowns because she always brought her own. She wasn't as easy or as pleasant as members of the Royal Family. My favourite actress Vivien Leigh was another patient. She had sprained her ankle and threw a tantrum when told she should not go on stage the next day. All the same I fell for her charm and beauty. She was really captivating and I found it difficult to take my eyes off her.

My work as a radiographer was all quite entertaining but hard work and we often had to work late. We were on call every other night. My salary was £2 per week. I was lucky to have many friends in London who took me to plays, films and dinner dances. I saw wonderful performances by actors such as Laurence Olivier, John Gielgud and Peggy Ashcroft. I worked hard and played hard. On one occasion I was driven after work to Cambridge where I changed into my ball gown. We had dinner in college, danced at the Trinity College Ball, and from there we gate-crashed into Clare College Ball. These balls had the leading bands of the day, such as Victor Silvester, Henry Hall and others playing many Gershwin and Fred Astaire favourites. We danced until we were exhausted. Then we would drift in a punt on the Backs – the river at Cambridge – before having breakfast at 6:00 am. At 7:00 am we drove back to London just in time for work. In my dazed, sleepy condition, I once forgot to put a film into fix so it all had to be repeated. One can behave recklessly at twenty-one.

My busy life-style caught up with me via a spastic colon – now called IBS – which led to an appendectomy. After the operation I needed to convalesce for some weeks. I left Graham-Hodgson's practice and moved to work at King's College Hospital which was more my scene. I really loved hospital work where there were people from all backgrounds and many patients needing reassurance and a kindly word. The doctors, nurses, radiographers and technicians were all interesting people.

Sir Harold Graham-Hodgson

HRH King George VI and Queen Elizabeth

On 12 May 1937, the Duke of York was crowned on the day set for his brother's coronation. He became King George VI and the Duchess, Queen Elizabeth. A wonderful elaborate procession wound its way from Buckingham Palace to Westminster Abbey. I was invited by one of my then boyfriends, John Hopper, to watch from a balcony in Pall Mall from where we looked down on the royal procession in all its glory. Just off the balcony was a large room with tables laden with champagne, caviar and rich truffles and every sort of delicacy. No one would have had a better view or experience of such an event. My first attempts at colour photography were made at that time – the results were under-exposed but they remind me of that special day.

In 1937, I joined my parents on their usual holiday to Cruden Bay Hotel. My school friend Mabel came with us. We were young, working women who enjoyed the company of young men. I had received offers of marriage but was in no hurry. I was waiting for the one who bowled me over.

In the Cruden Bay Golf Club challenge trophy of that year, a young chap of twenty six was playing. He was a brilliant international golfer. He had already won two silver salvers for the best amateur in the German Open Championship two years running. He had been at Oxford University studying PPE and had then gone up to Aberdeen University to read Psychology, but mostly he played golf. Whereas most golfers were staying at the hotel, Dick Walker, who was always unconventional, was staying in a disused horse-drawn caravan beside the golf course. I had seen him in

Dick, on the Cruden Bay Golf Course, practising his chipping

Dick

front of a huge mirror that was propped up against the caravan. In the mirror he watched himself swinging the golf club. I remember thinking that this was a curious thing to do. Little did I know then how important working in front of a mirror was to become.

I walked the golf course with Mabel and watched him play. Dick came up to us and said, 'The boys want me to ask you to tea but I shouldn't come because we have rats!' What an introduction. I believe that this was the very moment I fell in love with him (and that has never changed – my life took on a new route). Despite such an unpromising invitation, Mabel and I were undeterred and went for tea in the caravan. There we met more golfing enthusiasts but, thankfully, no rats.

Dick was nice-looking, with dark curly hair, a straight nose and a solemn expression. His appearance and face were reminiscent of a Modigliani portrait. He appeared to be serious-minded up to a point, but he also liked to shock people, especially his mother and aunts, by saying outrageous things.

My parents invited Dick to dinner at the Cruden Bay Hotel. Afterwards, we danced to gramophone records. Each evening we would meet and dance – the waltz, foxtrot, quick-step and tango. We loved the favourite dance music of the time – Lew Stone, Benny Goodman, Duke Ellington. The music was so full of rhythm and fun that one had to dance.

During this time Dick first told me about his lessons with Frederick Matthias Alexander (FM). He had read one of FM's books, *The Use of the Self*, particularly the section about golf and keeping your eye on the ball. He had gone to London to have some lessons before coming back to Scotland to apply FM's principles to his golf.

Following this holiday, Dick often came to stay with us at St Ives. We spent glorious days sailing on the river, playing golf and dancing. We shared a similar background and a love of outdoor pursuits and knew then that we wanted to spend our lives together. Dick introduced me to rock climbing. There was chemistry between us, that high electrical charge that struck to the soul and it was so precious that I always wanted to please him.

In September 1937, when I had my new job as radiographer at King's College Hospital, Dick persuaded me to have lessons with FM Alexander which I found most interesting, but I came away from my first lessons as stiff as a poker. At the time, I was living in Warwick Square near Victoria and Dick was staying at his mother's house in Kensington. Also staying there was his uncle Air Chief Marshal, Sir Wilfrid Freeman. He asked

First rock-climb   *Sir Wilfrid Freeman*

Dick & Elisabeth on Crib Goch, North Wales

Dick's mother why Dick did not get on with the job and marry me. Then Dick's mother offered us the top floor of her house in Gilston Road.

Dick and I both decided that we wanted to study the Technique. Dick joined FM Alexander's training course in early 1938 and I left King's College Hospital to join him. In order to undertake training, I had to take a part-time job which I did at the Hospital of St John and St Elizabeth (called Jack and Lizzie's) in St John's Wood. There I gave x-ray treatment to cancer patients. My days were very busy because I cycled from Kensington through Hyde Park and up to St John's Wood to my job and, after a morning's work, I'd cycle down to Ashley Place near Victoria to the training course and then back to Kensington at 5:00 pm. Looking back now this was quite a tough day.

Those days were so different from today. It was unusual then for a woman to be seen riding a bicycle. Trousers were not then in fashion so skirts or coats were worn on the bike. 'See your knickers, Miss' – a ribald jest from a passing lorry driver was the norm. It was only during the war that trousers, known as siren suits (sort of boiler suits) became allowable for women and, not until much later, were they worn at formal occasions.

Dick & Elisabeth's wedding

We got engaged in 1938, the day before Dick went off to climb in Russia. The following evening, in the theatre, my friends and former beaux offered their congratulations. Because the war was imminent, we decided to get married as soon as Dick's mother came back from America. We eventually married in November 1938 in Chelsea Old Church (later bombed in the war and rebuilt). It was a small wedding, largely family guests. We included Erika Whittaker, one of FM's assistants with whom Dick had made friends at his first visit to Ashley Place. Another of the assistants who was FM's niece, Marjorie Mechin, organised a gift of beautiful ivory handled knives from FM and the students. I wore a rather beautiful gown of oyster coloured velvet made by Nora Grove (not Madame Calista) and a veil of exquisite Honiton lace. The bridesmaids were two school friends. We held the reception at Dick's mother's house.

When we first went rock-climbing in North Wales we stayed at 'Ogwen' Cottage with Mrs Williams and her endless children, one born every year.

Dick on Crib Goch

Dick leading a climb

Eventually she sold the cottage to the climbing club and later to the Cottage Mountain Rescue team; in the 1960s it became the Ogwen Valley Mountain Rescue Organisation. Although I had climbed rocks in Yorkshire, the height and exposure of the climbs up the Lliwedd group of buttresses on Snowdon were a different challenge. I was determined to prove my ability to keep up with Dick, and to please him.

We spent our first, short honeymoon at the Pen-y-Pass Hotel in North Wales, another haven for rock climbers. Our honeymoon weekend was taken in November. We were the only people at the hotel; we had our meals in the snuggery in front of a roaring log fire. I remember it being so damp that you could wring water out of the eiderdown. In spite of that we found it very romantic; at least we could warm one another in bed. We did some difficult climbs; one climb was Lockwood's Chimney, a good climb to do on a wet day. Other climbs were on Tryfan and Idwal, most rated 'very difficult' by the climbing club – all were an exhilarating achievement. After doing most of the favourite climbs in North Wales we went on to climb in Europe. Throughout my time with Dick we chose to spend our holidays camping and in this way were able to discover many secluded and beautiful areas both in Europe and further afield.

Our campsite above Val d'Isère

My first serious mountain climb was in August 1939 when we went to the Alps with experienced climbers Graham Irving and his son Francis, and Gerald and Betts Palmer. They all stayed in a hotel in Val d'Isère, but Dick and I had our tent. After an evening meal with our companions we would walk up the hillside to our isolated camp. From the tent we looked down at the lights below and in the morning we awoke to beautiful views of the snow-capped mountains around us. There were no ski lifts in Val d'Isère then, only a simple village hotel. How things change. From there we climbed the mountains round Col d'Isèran, the Grand Sassière and walked up the Grand Motte which was snow-covered and very hard going as each foot went deep into the snow. We then drove to Breuil in Italy and Dick, Betts and I climbed the Matterhorn from the Italian side. The first men who managed to climb the Matterhorn were led by Edward Whymper in July 1865 when unfortunately four of the seven died on the way back (I played golf with Edward's brother Charlie in 1932 when he was eighty and I was eighteen years old).

We spent the night in the hut. I couldn't sleep and woke the others to say I'd heard German voices outside. They said, 'Oh, you've been dreaming.' But I knew I hadn't and after a while two men came into the hut.

Two views of Elisabeth above Val d'Isère

Elisabeth with Francis Irving, Betts Palmer and Graham Irving

Walking up to the Grande Motte

They needed food and water. They had been on the mountain for a day and a half. So we shared our food with them and they went to sleep but I didn't, I was far too excited. At dawn we continued up the mountain. At one point we took the wrong route and had great difficulty with all the snow and rocks finding the right way. A guide and his climber overtook us, going quite fast; obviously he had been there before. We reached the summit of the Matterhorn quite late. There was little time to enjoy the experience as we were anxious to return to Breuil where the rest of the party were expecting us. On the way down we had to hurry and I remember being in tears, I was so tired, I could barely move one leg after the other. It was a huge relief to drop safely back in bed in Breuil.

We had many excitements on this holiday. Dick and I wanted to go on to climb Mont Blanc, the highest mountain in Western Europe and probably the most beautiful and complex. Chamonix lies at its foot making it an accessible mountain; nevertheless it has claimed more lives than most others. Betts kindly lent us her car and we drove to Les Houches near Chamonix. Being well-acclimatised and fit, we soon climbed up to the first hut where we learned that, unfortunately, the weather was not good. We decided to proceed on up until it started snowing so hard we could barely see a foot in front of us. We arrived at a very small hut, only six feet long, but by this time we could barely see each other because the snow was falling so heavily. We rested in the hut for half an hour and then decided that we must go down. At this point avalanches were roaring down the mountainside. It was imperative to choose the right route to avoid these;

Hut on the Matterhorn, with Dick and Betts Palmer

this choice was based on observation and a little help from a useful guide-book which described the routes of the worst avalanches. We were fortunate to get down safely.

Back at the car in Les Houches, we found an envelope on the steering wheel. It was full of French francs and a note from Betts asking us to bring the car back home as she and Gez, her brother, had flown home. War, it seemed, was imminent. Dick and I drove down to Lake Annecy where he chose a five-star restaurant for a meal. This didn't suit me at all well after much exercise and little or no food. The next day I was really ill. Dick rowed me out on the lake for a change of scene hoping I would feel better but this did not help so we went to a bed-and-breakfast where I rested. While lying in bed Dick read to me an article about some German climbers attempting to be the first to reach the summit of the north face of the Eiger which is said to be the most treacherous climb in Europe. Many have lost their lives on that mountain. Identifying with those men created fear and adrenalin in me helping I believe to speed my recovery. I was still remembering our good fortune on the previous day having escaped the avalanches on Mont Blanc.

On our way home we drove through Paris where the French said, 'The English they have gone, you must go quickly too!' We got back home just three days before war against Germany was declared on 3 September 1939.

At the start of the war we lived at Gilston Road with Dick's mother and his uncle, Sir Wilfrid Freeman. Being in the Air Ministry and responsible for aircraft production, he was busily involved in efforts to win the war. His anxiety was obvious. Knowing how serious the situation was, he asked the Cabinet what plans they had. Chamberlain was dithering, the country uneasy and undecided about a new leader. It was not until May 1940 that Churchill became Prime Minister and played his part like an eloquent actor, rallying the country with his oratorical gifts. Our troops were sent to France and, in the first onslaught, our dentist 'Weedy' Green, who had bought the house in which we were born, and his brother-in-law were killed leaving his wife and two young sons. Soon after this our troops had to be rescued from Dunkirk.

In my teens I had seen films (*All Quiet on the Western Front* and *Journey's End*) portraying the horrors of the First World War and these had had a profound effect on me. So on that morning of 3 September 1939, the wailing of the air-raid warnings and the barrage balloons being raised above London made my heart sink. I couldn't believe there was to be war again.

*Dick's mother,
Josephine and his
uncle, Ralph Freeman
in 1939*

*Air Chief Marshal Sir Wilfrid Freeman (on the right) with Winston Churchill at a
meeting on board the HMS Prince of Wales in 1941*

Everyone was on the alert. When the Battle of Britain started, Marjory and Bill Barlow, FM Alexander's niece and her husband, brought their caravan into my parents' garden in St Ives, a refuge from London. Also, Marjory's sister Joan brought her daughter Jackie to lodge with friends of mine in St Ives. It was a worrying time.

While Dick was having an interview in Portsmouth for the Merchant Navy and I was playing tennis in Gosport with a cousin, there was suddenly a big air raid on Portsmouth and Gosport. My cousin and I went into a small shelter. This saved us from being killed by railings that were sent flying by the blast of a bomb on a military target nearby. This so shocked my digestive system that I felt nauseous all the time. The Gleadowes and their twins, Richard and Tess, who were friends in Calamansac in Cornwall took pity on me and invited me to stay with them for a short while. However, the smell of freshly caught mackerel which was their main diet increased my sickness. The most enjoyable and therapeutic part of my stay was lying on the deck of Merry Maid, their yacht, as we sailed out to sea. During an air raid in their area we all lay under the kitchen table, as our only refuge.

The House at Calamansac

At the beginning of the war Dick joined the London River Fire Service until he went into the Merchant Navy and then the Royal Naval Volunteer Reserve (RNVR). He worked in the engine room of the merchant ship *Azur* with Eric Hiscock (the famous sailing circumnavigator) which was in the Solent off Yarmouth, Isle of Wight. One weekend while visiting Yarmouth I met Mrs Merriman, wife of Captain Merriman, who had been bursar at Winchester College, Dick's school. On hearing of this connection she insisted that Dick should meet her husband. This was duly arranged with Dick in fear and trepidation. Captain Merriman said he was just the sort of man he wanted for taking over one of the private yachts which had been commandeered for examination of boats in the Solent (the old school tie being flourished yet again). In the meantime Dick was told to go and get a Yacht Master's Certificate with Captain Watts in London. From there, in May 1940, Dick brought a friend in a bowler hat to Gilston Road, where I was living with his mother, asking for bread and iron rations. They were joining the crowd of open boats towed across the Channel to go to the rescue of our troops in Dunkirk. Dick always made light of this experience but he did admit he felt seasick until they were dive-bombed and that cured it. In the small boats they picked up men from the beaches and took them to the bigger ships further out at sea.

The night before Dick's interview and eye test for joining the RNVR, we stayed with his uncle, Sir Wilfrid Freeman, in Berkeley Square. That night was the first big air-raid on the West End and the noise was really terrifying. The entire building shook and vibrated. Dick kept saying, 'I must sleep or I shan't pass my eye test tomorrow.' In the morning we saw the building next door had taken a direct hit. The wall was missing so that the baths and fireplaces were just hanging, disgorged from the ruined rooms. When walking along Piccadilly I was in floods of tears as I saw the huge craters in the middle of the road. The acrid stench of burning and smoke hung in the air, filling my nose with fumes of cordite mixed with wood ash. Beside the road, fires were still burning. We had had an unbelievably narrow escape.

Dick took command of the yacht *Llanthony* which was based in Yarmouth, Isle of Wight. He was told to choose his own crew and an interesting motley crew it was. He nearly had Dylan Thomas. The second-in-command was Anthony Cox who had previously trained cats in a circus. I joined Dick there as often as I could but I was still training with FM. I helped to paint and to camouflage the vessel. Captain Merriman, watching me from the bridge, asked jokingly: 'What do you pay the boy, vittels and no rum?' He entered into the spirit of it.

Merchant Ship Azur

HMS Llanthony

My first son, Julian, was born on 13 December 1941. When I was pregnant with him, I spent some time in a bedsit in Yarmouth on the Isle of Wight where Dick was stationed in command of HMS *Llanthony* from which he had to go aboard any ship entering the Solent to check its validity. Towards the end of my pregnancy I stayed in St Ives with my parents and arranged to have the baby at an evacuated maternity hospital in St Neots. When I started labour pains my father had to drive me those ten miles, he hoped I would not have the baby on the way; but he left me alone on a trolley at the hospital. I was there some time until a nurse decided to take me into the delivery room. Saying whispered 'ahs'* and having some gas and air I had an easy delivery.

At that time, after the birth, babies were not left with their mothers but put in a nursery and taken to their mothers five times a day for breast feeding. On one occasion when I was brought the wrong baby, I had a small room alone and had to shriek loudly to recall the nurse; I wondered

Dick with Julian at his christening   *Julian aged 5*

* See Chapter 9 for a description of whispered 'ahs'.

who was feeding mine. The place was really primitive and, as was the custom, I was kept in bed for two weeks, and was so thankful to go back to my parents and be with my baby. They adored their first grandson; they already had a granddaughter. When he was three months old, I took him south to see his father who was stationed in Yarmouth. This time I stayed in a house with another naval family and it was from here that Julian was christened.

I stayed in Yarmouth with Dick until, in December 1942, he was posted overseas. He had been given command of a Motor Torpedo Boat (MTB) in the Mediterranean where he stayed without returning for two and three-quarter years. I spent most of that time with my parents where Julian had a lot of freedom in their house and garden. He decided to make his sandpit look pretty with the heads of all my father's prize tulips from the driveway entrance, planting them in rows in the sand. He was also adventurous and, aged two, he disappeared to explore the local recreation ground. In August 1943, I gave birth to my second son Gavin at Fulmer Chase, a maternity home for officers' wives. I then returned to live with my parents in St Ives until 1945. Towards the end of the war Dick's mother found a house in Winchester for us to rent so that Dick would have a home to which to return, and with Julian aged three and Gavin one and a half, we moved there. Being very independent, Julian would tricycle along the pavement down the hill and around the block.

Julian and Gavin were very close – soulmates

After we had been in Winchester for six months, Dick returned from abroad. After such a long absence, to find he was the father of these two lovely boys aged four and two must have been a shock to him. For five years, before the war, Dick and I had been inseparable and obsessed with one another. Inevitably, after nearly three years apart, things were different. He had been having a dangerous and exciting time in the Mediterranean. Domestic life must have been dull in comparison. He now had two sons to care for but they were strangers to him. Our first quarrel was when he applied to go off to join the war effort in Japan. Fortunately he was not accepted but was given a shore job in Oxford until the end of the war.

It was a terribly cold winter in 1946 when we rented a house, next to Bill and Marjory Barlow who were also teaching the Alexander Technique, in Keats Grove, Hampstead. The Barlows had two children of the same age as ours. Hampstead Heath was covered with snow for some time. Gavin, normally very timid, loved tearing down slopes on a toboggan. We sent Julian to a Steiner school. He wasn't happy there and found his way back across Hampstead High Street, a big main road, to his home. The time he enjoyed most was playing with Gavin and the Barlow children, having some pre-school play from the teachers who rented the flat above our garage. They had great fun learning through play.

The house in Keats Grove was in a fashionable part of Hampstead, opposite Keats House. In order to have fresh eggs we kept hens in the back garden. We also had a poodle called Diana. Today, the area is so grand I am sure this would not be allowed. Following this pattern, wherever we lived as a family we had dogs, cats, hens and bantams.

Not being artists ourselves, Dick and I were hungry for many forms of art and we took every opportunity to indulge this pleasure whether sculpture, painting, architecture, photography or movement. In 1946 a friend gave us an introduction to Barbara Hepworth and Ben Nicholson, and we were invited to tea with them in their home in St Ives, Cornwall, also meeting their triplets. This gave us an added interest in the wonderful pieces of art they produced. Returning to St Ives recently I spent time in Barbara's studio and garden, bringing home to treasure the photos I was able to take. In our 1946 visit to St Ives we also met the potter Bernard Leach and he generously allowed us to watch him at work, sending us home with a memorial cereal bowl with his insignia.

By 1947, Dick and I had both finished our Alexander training and Dick had become one of FM's teaching assistants at Ashley Place. I was busy at home with two young children. Dick was not getting the intellectual stimulation from me that he needed. The intensity of our emotional relation-

*One of Barbara
Hepworth's fine
works*

ship had been lost during those years of separation and this upset me a lot
at the time. We were no longer that inseparable couple though, with later
children and our common interests, we recovered much of the closeness.

In the summer of 1947, when I was pregnant with Mark, Dick and I
had a holiday in Switzerland. We drove in an elderly car on bomb-dam-
aged roads still suffering from the war. I hoped that the jolting would not
bring on a premature birth. We camped by the lake near Interlaken. I had
a lilo to sleep on but I was disturbed in the night by the drumming of
mice scratching underneath so I preferred to sleep on the ground. Villag-
ers came down from the hills laden with fruit and vegetables which they
insisted we should share. They also provided us with fresh goat's milk.
There are too many wonderful occasions to recount but Dick's comment
at the end of these holidays was, 'When can we come again?'

Our two boys frequently suffered from colds and the medics advised
tonsillectomies. This was a common operation at the time so we arranged
to have them done in Cambridge near my parents' home. That time for
me was a real nightmare. While they were in theatre having the operation,
I was sent out of the building only to return to find them back in their
beds. Julian was spitting blood. I called the nurse. He was taken back to
theatre where he died. I believe he drowned in his own blood. One of the

Camping at Interlaken

medics made the mistake of saying, 'I see you have another on the way.' How little he understood the depths of emotion after the loss of a child.

Dick was away teaching in Cardiff so we were not able to comfort one another at this painful time. Gavin and I went to stay with my parents at Hemingford Grey where the funeral took place and Dick eventually arrived in time.

Gavin, who was twenty months younger than Julian, was profoundly affected by his death. He had lost his friend and his role model and I his mother, out of grief and ignorance, pretended nothing had happened, and so instead of protecting this suffering child the situation came about where he became anxious. Nowadays one would get help and support in bereavement. When Gavin was grown up, he told me that he blamed himself for his brother's disappearance. This taught me the importance of sharing our thoughts and emotions with our children from the earliest age.

When our third son, Adrian (Mark) was born at home in October 1947, he arrived very quickly on the teaching table. He had a block of mucous across one bronchus which was affecting his breathing and thanks to a wonderful midwife who insisted on holding him upright day and night giving him oxygen, he survived. During this time, I was not allowed to help as, after childbirth, one was kept in bed for two weeks. Fortunately, in 1957 when Lucia was born, I was not kept in bed at all.

While she was holding Mark, that wonderful midwife looked out the window and saw a pram in the garden backing onto ours. In this pram was

Mark's Baptism: Elisabeth, with Anthony Furse and Liz Freeman (godparents) and Canon Adam Fox (Dean of Westminster)

Anthony, the son of Lee Miller and Roland Penrose, who had been born a month before Mark. Lee Miller had been a famous war photographer and Roland was a surrealist artist and collector. Mark was invited to Anthony's first birthday party and Dick and I were invited into their house in Downshire Hill, Hampstead. For art lovers like us, this was better than any other picture gallery having so many originals of Picasso, Braque, Miró: name it, they were there. Dick was in his element. Lee gave me photographs she took of Mark and Anthony at that birthday party in 1948. We lost touch with them when we went South Africa at the end of that year. Recently, I got in touch with Anthony and he generously showed me round his parents' home, Farley Farm, which had become a museum of their work and treasures. I also had the opportunity to see an exhibition of Lee's excellent photographic work.

Mark (right) with Anthony Penrose (left)

E with Tony Penrose

FM noticing a pupil's breathing

F M Alexander

3 FM Alexander Training

On first meeting FM Alexander in 1937, I was struck by his twinkling eyes, his freedom of movement and general poise. His rather old-fashioned dress and spats reminded me so much of my paternal grandfather – an archetypal English gentleman. Immediately he put me at ease, and all through that first lesson, which was largely sitting and standing using his elegant chair, he referred to me as 'little lady'. The lesson was amazing. His hands seemed to draw me right up out of the chair. I felt like a different person, but I tried holding on to it. This is a danger about which we teachers must warn our pupils. I had not learned then that the process of inhibiting, thinking and directing is the essence of the work. It is not the changed posture that is important, but the stopping of our habitual interference with our use, balance and coordination.

FM referred to his principles as the 'Work'. He and others never liked the word 'technique' but it seems to have been adopted. I like to think of it as a thinking tool to help us in our daily activities.

Often it is difficult for new pupils to understand the 'non-doing' aspect of the Work, which is about thinking and directing and re-educating the nervous system. Today everyone is in a hurry so that taking more time to be aware and to stop habitual responses is difficult. What Alexander termed the 'primary control' is the free balance of the head on the atlanto–occipital joint at the top of the spine. FM qualified this by saying that

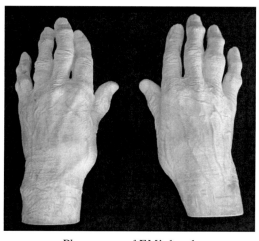

Plaster casts of FM's hands

there is no primary control as such; it becomes something in the sphere of relativity and is a master reflex in coordinating the whole psychophysical organism. He said that it was an essential prerequisite for satisfactory functioning. We need good balance and coordination for our general well-being but this gets interfered with by stress and by lengthy sitting at desks and computers.

Alexander's discovery was unique and so basic – it is vital that its fundamental simplicity is not lost in application to any activity. His teaching is so simple yet one's habit patterns make it difficult to use. The teaching is clear: it is taking time to stop one's habitual way and allowing one's neck to be free so the head is leading and freely balancing at the top of the spine, with the back lengthening and widening. This is the essence of Alexander's teaching and it is an approach which can be used in all of life's activities.

Sir Stafford and Dame Isobel Cripps wanted to help FM set up an Alexander society. In 1947 some Ashley Place teachers including Dick and I joined the Crippses and FM to discuss the possibilities. FM was always wary that his discoveries would not be kept pure – that they would be misinterpreted or adulterated so, in spite of much discussion, he would not agree to starting a society of teachers. The Crippses then gave their support to Charles Neil at Lansdowne Road which did not please FM

FM on his eightieth birthday entertaining Lady Isobel and Sir Stafford Cripps

as Charles was teaching his own version of the Work of which FM disapproved. This caused a rift with the Crippses though Sir Stafford and Dame Isobel did accept an invitation to FM's eightieth birthday celebration at which Sir Stafford gave a speech praising FM and his work.

It was in 1958, well after FM's death, that the Society of Teachers of Alexander Technique (STAT) was formed. In 1992, with different entry criteria, the Alexander Technique International (ATI) which is a worldwide organisation of AT teachers, students and supporters, came into being.

People often ask me what FM would think of the Technique today. We can't possibly know. The Work is about freedom to change and we teachers must stick to his principles in applying the Work in our individual ways of teaching, whether it be to musicians, dancers, singers, actors or to people in other walks of life with different interests. Today the Work is valued all over the world. It is basic to our well-being.

When I first started training at Ashley Place in early 1938, there were about fifteen students on the course. Dick had started training a few months before me. We were, I suppose, the second intake. When I started, Walter Carrington was also a student. Among the other students there were Eric de Peyer, Alma Frank and Lilly Hellstenius; Bill Barlow joined some months later.

FM, who was seventy that January, came in to the teaching room where we were gathered round in a circle. He would work with us for an hour or

Jerusalem 1996 - friends with whom Elisabeth trained.
Erika Whittaker, Elisabeth, Dilys and Walter Carrington and Marjory Barlow

so each afternoon, giving each of us the experience of his great direction. Other teachers would follow him round as he worked with us and they too would give us 'turns'. It was always lively and enjoyable. FM would entertain us by talking about the work or ask us questions such as: 'What is inhibition?' Sometimes he would talk of other things that were of interest in the day: for example, he referred to John Dewey (the American philosopher) and George E Coghill (the eminent scientist) and explained how they confirmed his findings. If he saw us getting too worried or intense he would make us run around the block to keep psycho-physically active. He used to say, 'You've got to think. It's the thinking that counts.' He also said, 'Learn the principles and teach your students to do so.' All that was quite foreign to us as beginners.

Our teaching room was usually cold for in those days there was no central heating. In winter, a coal fire was lit at one end of the double room. There was no table and lying on the floor was not very attractive. I often wore a coat. When we first started training, my mother-in-law disapproved of the way we sat. In those days we wore skirts and, with Alexander, we weren't allowed to cross our legs; we were meant to allow the knees to go away from each other. Lying on the floor or on the table we used to put modesty cloths over our knees.

After class at four o'clock, a group of us would sometimes go out to tea at the local Lyons tea shop. Sometimes we even went to the more expensive Fullers, a real treat, especially for the walnut cake. Over tea there was lots of Alexander talk and sharing of experiences. Sometimes Dick and I would be invited by FM to tea in his basement dining room. He insisted on making the tea himself, a good China tea, and we usually ate his favourite caraway seed cake which we had bought from a shop in South Kensington. On occasions he would offer us Balkan Sobranie cigarettes. In those days it was quite acceptable to smoke. We would talk about current affairs, who would win the Derby and his views on the impending war. FM once came to dinner with us at Keats Grove – he arrived by taxi on his own. He liked good food, yet I remember that I gave him crab salad followed by a cheese souffle that rose so much it stuck to the top of the oven. All the same he was most appreciative. He also mentioned some of his current pupils including the actor, Robert Donat (his young family sometimes came with him).

I found FM to be a very compassionate man. He was most supportive to us after our son Julian died.

Albert Redden (AR), FM's brother, spent a lot of time in America but when he was in London, he taught on the course. He was very helpful in answering simple, seemingly silly questions in a totally generous, non-judgemental way. FM did not like to answer questions about the Technique. He said, 'You must read the books.' And he would show by his hands-on work the answer to the question.

I learnt a lot from all the assistant teachers on the training course: Pat Macdonald (who was a bit of terror with the ladies), Marjory Barlow, Irene Stewart and Erika Whittaker, some of whom had trained on FM's first course (1931–1934). Walter Carrington, who completed his training in 1938, was always a dedicated teacher and a great help to first-year students. Ethel Webb, Erika's aunt, gave me great lying-down turns on the floor. FM called these 'inhibition work'. There was no table in the students' room. Teaching is such an individual thing. Sometimes one responds better to one person than another. Margaret Goldie, one of FM's main assistants, didn't teach in class at that time although she was very supportive to FM and taught at his little school at Penhill. Irene Stewart was a lovely, warm Scottish woman who was quite deaf. She and Erika would work a lot together. She came to stay at St Ives and we had great fun together, boating on the river. It was an enjoyable time, and although sometimes a student might criticise another saying, 'You're pulling down', or 'You're pulling your head back', in general the atmosphere was good.

It took nine years for me to complete my training. As the war came closer it brought disruption to Ashley Place and Penhill. In July 1940 FM sailed to North America with Ethel Webb, Margaret Goldie and Irene Stewart, and eventually re-established his teaching there. I was invited to go with him but I didn't for a moment seriously consider leaving my family. Three months after FM sailed for America, a bomb fell close to 16 Ashley Place. Thankfully no one was injured but Walter Carrington and Marjory Barlow, who had continued to teach there, closed the house. Walter and other assistant teachers joined the war effort: Bill Barlow went to be an Army doctor, Walter and Patrick joined the RAF, and Dick joined the RNVR. It wasn't until September 1945 that Alexander training began again. Then there were nine or so new students, including Tom Davidson and Guy Baron, a couple who were most supportive and became good friends, and Duncan Whittaker who married Erika. Many others joined in the following months including Peter Scott who was a pianist and had a large family who lived nearby. He went on to run his own successful training school.

Training in the Work was all-consuming. Before the war Dick and I and had been carefree and had enjoyed ballroom dancing almost every evening after training – either at the Hammersmith Palais de Dance or the

Astoria Dance Salon. And, looking back, it seems amazing that the roads were clear enough for us, on light evenings, to roller-skate round Kensington and the Boltons. We led such active lives. At weekends we would go rock-climbing in North Wales. We had married in 1938 and afterwards had the responsibility of bringing up our young children. In order to go in each day to complete my training, I had to have baby-sitters. Walter and Dilys Carrington's and Marjory and Bill Barlow's children were born around much the same time.

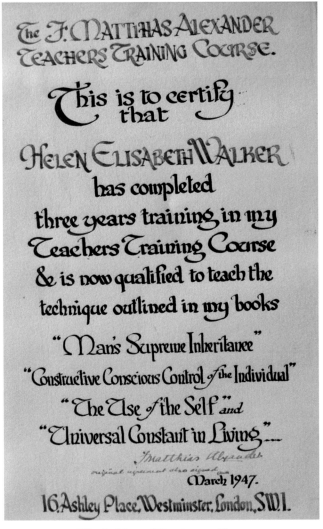

The F. Matthias Alexander Teachers Training Course.

This is to certify that

Helen Elisabeth Walker

has completed three years training in my Teachers Training Course & is now qualified to teach the technique outlined in my books

"Man's Supreme Inheritance"
"Constructive Conscious Control of the Individual"
"The Use of the Self" and
"Universal Constant in Living"...

Matthias Alexander

March 1947.

16, Ashley Place, Westminster, London, SW1.

Elisabeth's qualification certificate

4   Fantastic Journey

In 1948 Irene Tasker, who taught the Alexander Technique in Johannesburg, decided to leave South Africa. FM suggested to Dick that it might be a good plan for us to go and teach there. Dick, who was always out for a challenge, decided to travel overland across France, Spain, Morocco, Algeria, Sahara, Nigeria, French Equatorial Africa, Uganda, Kenya, Tanzania, Northern and Southern Rhodesia and on to Johannesburg.

This was at a very difficult time in my life. It was up to me to use Alexander's teaching of inhibiting and directing to think. I've always had a huge love of children – my own or others – so it was particularly difficult to leave our five-year-old and one-year-old sons. This was an enormous decision for me. We could not take the children on this hazardous journey but I felt it was so important to keep our marriage together and go with Dick. My wonderful mother-in-law, always a great support, suggested leaving the children with her and a young nanny who would bring them out later by sea. It was heart-rending but it was the best answer.

We started planning in September 1948. Dick bought an ex-army three ton lorry with four-wheel drive. Our intention was to climb in the Hoggar Mountains and in the Ruwenzori and Mount Kenya. Another keen mountaineer joined us, his name was Nick Wollaston. Then we found Sam, who had been a tank driver in the Irish Guards – and he was an invaluable mechanic and a good cook. He brought his friend Judd and I was there too.

The preparations were endless – maps, visas and permits to cross the Sahara, stores and special equipment with emphasis on petrol, water, oats, bully-beef and potatoes, all sharing space with paraffin for the primus stove, bedding and limited supplies of clothing. Dick and I planned to sleep in the lorry, the others in their own tent.

We set off on 1 January 1949, through France heading for the Pyrenees. We arrived at the Spanish frontier after dark and the guards were not happy to be disturbed. Our training in inhibition was put to the test here as the lorry was meticulously searched. Two shotguns and a rifle were discovered which convinced them that we were there to stir up a revolt. None of us spoke Spanish but after much sign-language and several bottles of wine we softened their mood and convinced them that the guns were for obtaining flesh or fowl for food, as well as for our self-protection. At last it was agreed to have the firearms sealed in a large box and not opened

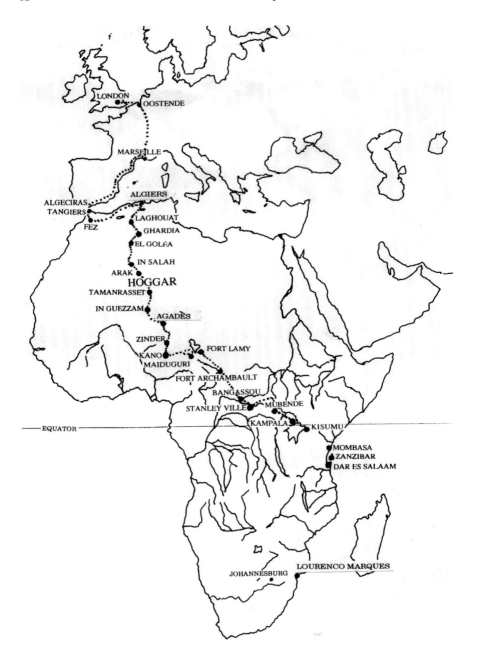

Route of overland journey across Africa in 1949

till we had left the country. To find a local carpenter to do this at 11:30 pm was amazing and we were lucky to leave the frontier after a three hour hold-up.

Fully laden truck at Calais

Dick and the 'crew' in Spain: Nick, Sam and Judd

We drove along the Spanish coast, camping at night on moonlit beaches washed by the phosphorescent breakers of the Mediterranean, heading for Africa.

Malaga, Spain

Darling Mother and Father,

I find it almost impossible to write letters as there is not time between driving, eating, clearing up and sleeping. We get up at 6:00 am and try and get under way by 7:00 am, drive on until lunch time then on again until 7:00 or 8:00 pm – more food, clear up, bed, etc. We are having a wonderful time. It was very cold in France and I was very pleased indeed with the lambswool coat, it was just what I needed. All the time we've been in Spain it has been wonderful weather rather like lovely days in England. We bathed in the Mediterranean the first time we saw it four days ago.

I can't get over the miles and miles of orange groves absolutely laden with fruit, there are also, of course, lots of lemons and grapefruit, wish I could send you some. They are all dropping off the trees. I picked up one I thought looked like a Seville, Dick and I managed to eat it but it was sour. I think Spain is a wonderful country, we haven't been through any dull parts at all – usually mountains with attractive little villages composed usually of neat white cottages. We've been along the coast most of the time and the sea has been unbelievably blue.

We are very lucky in our crew, they are all so nice. The engineer is quite excellent and has earned his keep many times over already. The reason I'm managing to write this is that they are changing a wheel. We have just had lunch. I am having to sit in the shade as I was too hot in the sun. I should think this is the nicest time of year here as everything is that light, fresh green, tomatoes ripening in the fields, green peas and broad beans in flower, also the almond and peach trees in blossom. You would love it so.

We are feeding ourselves well, most of them have terrific appetites and of course we can have oranges either for the asking or for about 2d a lb. I'm feeling very spoilt to be here at all, it really is a wonderful life, this gypsy existence. The Spanish people are all friendly and nice, they seem to live a pleasant, unhurried life even if they are a bit primitive in some respects. They amble around with their donkeys or collect round the village fountain to gossip. If we stop anywhere in the towns we collect a vast crowd – all stand around and stare open-mouthed.

Well the tyre is back again now. So I must stop. When I write again we shall, I expect, be in North Africa or the desert where it won't be so interesting but it's all very exciting.

You would adore all the baby kids and lambs, they are so sweet – the children carry the very young ones.

Very much love, Beth

Donkey carts were the main form of transport in Spain. Driving through one small town the iron wheel-hub of a cart punctured one of the lorry's 50-gallon tanks and petrol poured onto the road. A crowd gathered to witness our plight. A tram passed with people puffing and flicking their cigarettes – all most alarming. It was miraculous we left without catching fire.

All through Spain military patrols stopped us to examine our papers and to assure themselves that we weren't revolutionaries. At Gibraltar we arranged for a boat to take us from Algeciras to Tangiers – another of the many occasions to put FM's teaching into practice. The lorry had to be lifted on davits and then swung over the sea twenty feet below. We stood hoping all four wheels would reach the deck of the boat as it was swung and lowered; they took several attempts before succeeding. All of it was quite nerve-wracking. On arrival at Tangiers the lorry had to be disembarked in the same way. I'm grateful today to have the 'drive-on, drive-off' method for vehicles.

Spanish donkey cart

Loading the lorry at Algeciras

After a short time in Tangiers we spent our first night in Africa in Morocco and then drove on through dusty avenues of Eucalyptus trees to Fez – a delightful town with fortified gateways, narrow streets and colourful beggars. Dick bought a beautiful bowl there which we gave away in Johannesburg, where I hope it is being appreciated.

We had to go on to Algiers to buy a special permit to cross the Sahara and to have the lorry examined to check if it could stand the strain. We put all our documents, carnet de passage and passports together with petrol coupons in one briefcase as these all had to be examined by the commandant at every town. We had to report on arrival and couldn't proceed until these had all been cleared.

Algiers 30 January, 1949

Darling Mother and Father,

Thank you so much for your three letters I got here on Thursday when we arrived. We have had a wonderful trip up to date and have been lucky here to have got through all the necessary business in two days. Many people are here a month or more – they say we make our way South today. It is 8:00 am, we are waiting for the rest of the party who have had a night out at an hotel. Dick and I slept in the truck on the beach. The truck makes a most comfortable self-contained bedroom.

The souk at Fez

I have been furious with myself with not writing to you for your birthday. I thought so much about it beforehand and then when I joined the 'trekkers' we were pressing on so fast that I forgot to even try to make time but I think about you so much which is almost as good as writing. Please write to me again – air letter to Poste Restante, Kano, British Nigeria.

It is so lovely hearing from you when I'm so far away.

We should be in Kano in about three weeks. Air letters here take two to four days. After Kano, Poste Restante, Nairobi.

I am so thrilled and excited by all these places. Fez was a most attractive Arab town and we spent a short while in the market place in the Arab quarter, it was amazing.

Algiers is very attractive in an entirely different way. People have been so kind here especially the 'Shell' people who have taken us around in their cars, had us to drinks in the evening, introduced us to a well-know mountaineer. Altogether we've been most lucky.

Please give Stuart and Joy and Pip and José my love and news till I have time to write. I thought there would be time here but these two days we have been much involved in preparations, visas and all such necessities and of course we want to get away as soon as we can. Almost all the work of organising and provisioning falls on Dick and me (even to the provision of toilet paper). They are nice lads but they have [not] got in the way of doing all that sort of thing so we've had a lot of shopping to do as well as all the official work. It is thought an excellent party and all are out to make the best of things.

All my love, Elisabeth

At last we were free to drive south. The road climbed up a rocky gorge with colonies of little grey monkeys swarming about the cliffs and through fertile hills with farms and vineyards. Ragged children ran beside us cheering us on as we reached La Laghouat, a town with a European population and well-cultivated gardens. From there on we were in desert and clouds of dust and yellow sand were sucked into the back of the lorry as we rattled along a rough corrugated track. The lorry did not have the power to ride these. Sand was everywhere, in our eyes, ears, nostrils. We all became sand-coloured. Water was precious; we waited for an oasis before washing. When the days became less cold and the air was warm enough to open the covers and have a through draught, it was more comfortable. At this point we were overtaken by some Belgians driving quite fast in a high-powered car which could ride the corrugation while our slower moving vehicle had to bump on every ridge.

North Sahara

Being in the desert, surrounded by nothing but sand and seeing the horizon in every direction, shows so clearly the planet earth. We could see the sun rising and setting and often we thought there was water ahead but mirages were deceiving. Being the only woman with three men about I had to leave all sense of modesty and squat over a hole I had dug in the sand when nature called. It was all an endurance test but a fantastic experience.

The most attractive oasis town was El Golea with its huge date palms and Cypresses and handsome, white-painted houses. We drank and ate at the hotel decorated with hand-woven rugs. At the bar were French officers in military jackets and large blue silk trousers sipping cognac and smoking Gauloises. It all seemed like a fancy dress party.

El Golea 3 February, 1949

This is the most beautiful oasis town – so peaceful and lovely. Palm trees, cyprus and orange and very attractive buildings and no form of transport other than a donkey or camel. So far we have done two stages of desert travel – most exciting and very beautiful but of course very uncomfortable. Rocks and deeply corrugated roads over which high powered cars go fast but we are forced to go about 10 mph. The truck is standing up to it all thanks to C and W's Garage, St Ives, and Sam's attentions since. We are most grateful for the locker which holds things in place well (and they take some holding as the bumping is unbelievable) and makes a most comfortable bed. The primus too is standing up to a great deal

El Golea

of use. It has had to have an overhaul on two occasions but has cooked us some excellent meals.

We have had colder weather in the desert than anywhere – 4° to 5° frost at night and some difficulty defrosting the windscreen and ourselves at 5.45 am. The sun rises at 6:30 am. and soon becomes pleasantly warm, the sun going down again at 5.30pm – glorious red sunsets. The sand is all colours and the scenery changes from hard rock peaks to soft sand dunes, from flat plains to valleys. We spent two days coming from the last oasis.

I hear we are now due off again from here so I must stop and post this while I've got the chance as it may be some days before we see a post-box.

Lots and lots of love,

Beth

From El Golea the track climbs over the Tademait Plateau rising hundreds of feet. The going was rough and stony. We constantly saw mirages ahead, believing we were approaching lakes of water only to be disappointed to find yet more sand and the endless and whole circular horizon. We descended sharply from the plateau round dangerous turns to Insalah, which looked like a child's toy fort. We bought camel meat and a type of bread baked in the sand – very gritty.

From Insalah the track enters the rugged, picturesque gorges of Arak. Some sections are very difficult but we eventually arrived at Tamanrasset with red and orange buildings and lines of pink tamarisk trees.

Tamanrasset is surrounded by the Hoggar Mountains, a range of rocky peaks rising to 9,000 ft, and as our aim was to climb Mount Ilamane, we reported to the commandant and drove towards the mountains, negotiating dried-up river beds and undulating zigzag tracks till we were forced to a halt with spectacular views of these arid mountains. The highest peak is Asekrem beside which was the hermitage of Père de Foucault, a Trappist monk. His hermitage has now become a tourist attraction with campsites and car-parks and a road to reach it. But in 1949 we had the whole area to ourselves. We camped here before starting our climb up Mount Ilamane.

It was bitterly cold when we set off at dawn to walk up through the rocks and scree to the foot of the mountain with ever changing colours as the sun rose. The climb was precipitous, but Dick was an experienced mountaineer and Nick and I were roped. We had to be aware of loose rocks but in due course we reached the summit where among stones on a cairn was an old biscuit tin with the names of the first party to reach the top. We added our names and we then began the equally difficult descent, disturbing a huge brown eagle unused to human company.

Tamanrasset

Mt. Ilamane

Hoggar Mountains

Mountain stream

The following is an account of the climb up Mount Ilamane, written by Nick Wollaston:

In Algiers, Dick the leader had called on an ex-Chamonix guide, M Frison Roche, a climber who had done some exploration in the Hoggar before the war. He had recommended Ilamane as the finest peak and the finest climb in the range, and had said that the only known route to the summit was up 'easy' chimneys on the north-east side as far as the conspicuous shoulder on the north ridge, and then up the steep arête itself. Scrambling up the screes on the south side we looked up at the terrific perpendicular bastions hanging over us in festoons of giddy cracks and slabs, and wondered whether we had come to the right mountain. Cliffs 1000ft. high plunged down from the sky like a great, silent, grey Niagara; a splendid playground for rock-climbing gymnasts with bunches of pegs and a sackful of hammers, but hardly the sort of route that we fancied to the top of our peak.

We stumbled round the foot of the cliffs to the east sound and here found that things looked a little easier; a wide terrace ran horizontally across the face, about half-way up, and seemed to join the northern arête at the very shoulder we were trying to reach. To get to the terrace, however, was difficult; we tied on the rope and started up a narrow gulley, Dick leading, but very soon found that what we were climbing was in no way what I should call a succession of 'easy' chimneys; rather was it a series of overhangs which, though dry, abounded in treacherous loose stones and crumbling rocks.

Dick led admirably, while I fumbled and cursed behind him, and the third man*, to my embarrassment, came up like a lift, with no difficulty. I was definitely not happy, and wondered what on earth the [ridge] was going to be like if this was supposed to be easy. When at last we reached the terrace we spread ourselves out and brought out the lunch. I timidly suggested that we might spend a pleasant afternoon lying there in the sun, with far less chance of breaking our necks than if we pursued our crazy attempt on the ridge, which must, I argued, be at least 50 times as hard as the few pitches we had already climbed; and anyhow, I said, how were we going to get down? Better not leave it too late…

But Dick was horribly full of confidence, and leaving us sitting on the rocks eating chocolates and dates, he disappeared for a little reconnoitring. Ten minutes he came back with a smirk on his face and the news that we had reached the terrace by the wrong route, and that there really was an easy way.

We scrambled along the terrace to the shoulder and looked up at the arête. It looked steep, but sound, and Dick led up the first pitch. The rock was warm and dry, a happy contrast with the cold, wet gully on a cliff in North Wales where Dick and I had been climbing only two months earlier. In Wales the wind had howled down the gully, the rain had trickled obstinately down my collar, and my fingers had been numbed by the stiff wet rope; but here the sun was shining and our feet would be dry when we got back to camp.

Nowhere in the climb was there any choice of route; the narrow ridge was flanked by cliffs that would obviously defy all attempts. Far away down to our right we could see the little white dots that marked our tents, and beyond them the track to Tamanrasset rolling away across the hills and finally losing itself in the haze and dazzle of the desert. At the top of the second pitch, Dick found a steel piton driven into a crack, and 50 feet higher was another with a rope sling, bleached and rotted, threaded through the ring. After about 200 feet of splendid climbing and another 100 feet of scrambling over loose rocks, we reached the cairn on top.

---

* Referring to me.

Summit of Mt. Ilamane

Tamanrasset 12 February, 1949

Dearest Joy [i.e. my sister-in-law],

We are having a truly wonderful time, I can't think how I could have had any doubts about coming. It is all very interesting and most of the country is very beautiful. It is very uncomfortable travelling in the desert most of the time and at times one feels one can't bear to be shaken and bumped any longer but the desire to press on and see more exciting things and more lovely country carries one through. I adore these Oasis towns with the Arabs sitting about the road selling bread, meat or oranges, and the little dark skinned children (they are nearly black round here) mainly Berbers and Tauregs.

We are having a couple of days off here while the truck is being overhauled. Dick and another lad and I have just climbed Ilamane, a very steep mountain in the Hoggar group. We were the third party to get up, the first British. I was the first woman. It was very steep but not as difficult as we expected. It is rather a joy to be able to stay in a nice place. We have been through so many places that we would like to stop several days at. As it is though I shall have to go on ahead from Nairobi in order to get to Jo'burg a bit before the children arrive and look round for a house. We know someone who has a very nice house who is coming home for good but it is doubtful whether we could afford it. Will you write to me: – c/o Mrs Whitcombe, c/o Barclays Bank, Nairobi, Kenya, and tell me Marguerite's address, also the people you knew in Cape Town and anyone else. Oh, yes, and John and Margaret's whereabouts. Even if I can't visit them Dick could on his way south. Do write and tell me all your news. I can't start to tell you mine really, it all has to be seen to be believed. We've already done over 4,000 miles in this lorry but in experience and the different people, ways of living, climate and other things, we seem much further away from England.

Masses of love to you both and the children, Beth

PS I am sitting in a pair of shorts, it is hot out of the wind but the dish-cloth froze solid in the truck last night.

Continuing south towards Zinder and Agadès it was difficult to find the route. We had been advised to follow tyre tracks left by the food lorries but often found ourselves confronting a large sand hill. We had to negotiate many sand drifts and sometimes resorted to using sand boards to stop dropping further into the sand. Often by all pushing we could move a few yards at a time. The driver was grinding on foot by foot in four-wheel drive.

As days and nights got warmer we were able to sleep on the soft sand at night and enjoy the silence and watch shooting stars. One night we were woken by a jackal rummaging in the lorry. We could not afford to share

Sand dunes in the Southern Sahara

our precious rations but it soon ran off when it realised we were around. It must have come many miles, as there was no available food or water in that area.

In Guezzam 15 February, 1949

Darling Mother and Father,

We are through most of the desert now and are having a most interesting and exciting time. It has suddenly got quite a lot warmer and we are sleeping out underneath the stars. The moon was so bright the first night it kept me awake and at 3:30 am a fox came and took a look at us, it had a look in the truck and then stood staring at me – it was only about 20 yards away and I woke Dick to show him and he stayed up for several seconds and then made off. Today we set off at 6 am and about half an hour later we saw a gazelle and as the boys were so keen to have a shot at something so I crept round to the back and told them, and Sam (the engineer) fired at him from the back of the truck and got him first time. I hated it, they are such attractive animals. We have seen about 20 of them today, one was on the road (track rather) and started running beside us but soon overtook us and crossed our bows doing about 40 mph, at least, and did look beautiful.

For two days the going was very sandy and several times we had to push but we avoided using our sand channels though once or twice it was a very close thing in bottom gear ratio just about holding our own. At Tamanrasset we met an English-man who had been broken down in the desert for 14 days – he was looking very sorry for himself, poor man.

Taureg and camel

We have met huge caravans of 2–300 camels looking most attractive and some of the Arabs are incredibly handsome. It is very difficult to make one another understand as they shout Arabic at the top of their voices and we shout French and no one gets much further.

<u>*Two days later.*</u>

We have come several hundred miles further south since I started this letter and we are now out of the desert and on our way to Kano where I shall be able to post this – looking forward to getting some letters there too.

There is a sudden change in the population here where they are mostly very dark skinned West Africans in very small amounts of clothing, whereas the last place we saw people they were mainly Arabs with as much clothing as possible with only their eyes showing.

There is so much to tell you but I cannot possibly get it into a letter. I think about you so much and long to know all that is happening. I think so often how you would enjoy the sun and how Pa would love the trip.

A Belgian has just come up to us, he has crossed the desert on the way to the Congo. He had a burst tyre and one of his party is in hospital with a broken neck. We have been lucky to have had no trouble but it really wasn't very tough.

All love, Beth

Village north of Kano

As we approached Agadès, the desert gave way to bush and wisps of scrubby grass. At one time a gazelle appeared running beside us, soon outpacing us, and small quails scurried through the sand.

At last we reached Kano after 6,000 miles, seven weeks from home, three weeks in the desert. The men must have been hungry. In 1949 there were colonial English in Africa who were generous and hospitable and always keen to meet people from England with news from home. In Kano we were invited to stay by one of these and given our first sit-down dinner in seven weeks. We enjoyed our two days rest with this delightful District Commissioner and his wife while repairs were done to the battered lorry.

We set off refreshed, heading due east towards Maiduguri but a hundred miles on we broke both front springs. Dick and I managed to hitch a lift back to Kano on a peanut lorry. Those hundred miles were the most uncomfortable of the whole 9,000 mile trip. The heat was so intense and without water we got very dehydrated. We could not risk cooling off in the occasional streams for fear of bilharzia.* How we welcomed the sun going down.

---

*   A serious parasitic infection with unpleasant symptoms picked up by swimming in affected water.

Arriving back in Kano we phoned the DC but he was out. Standing around wondering where to spend the night, we were approached by a local who invited us to stay with him. Next morning we visited the DC who welcomed us with great warmth and called his servant to bring refreshments saying he had some important visitors. The servant arrived and burst out laughing to see us again so soon. Having found new springs in Kano – they cost £15 – we managed to hitch a lift back at night and rejoined the men and the lorry. Sam had enjoyed cooking over a campfire, making a stew of guinea fowl and fresh vegetables they had managed to scrounge. It was faintly flavoured with sand and engine oil.

Kano 24 February, 1949

Darling Mother and Father,

I was so delighted to get all your letters when we arrived in Kano, a bit embarrassed to find though that they have been handed round to family as they have all been rather bad letters just scribbled off when I have been waiting in the truck for a petrol fill-up or some similar business. This is the first time I have sat down comfortably to write so you must make allowances! I keep wishing as I sit in the truck that I could be writing then and telling you all that was going on. I will now tell you about our experiences in Kano. We arrived here on Saturday, the 19th, at about 4 pm. One of the party had an introduction to the London and Kano Trading Co. and went to visit them whereupon they insisted that the whole party should be put up during our stay in Kano and they would take no refusal. Dick and I stayed with the Manager and his wife and the other three with the second-in-command. I have never met such hospitality. I unfortunately had to stay in bed on the Sunday with what they said was 'Kano tummy'. However, I was made to feel so much at home it did not matter. They said it was a good reason for our staying longer! Actually we could not leave on the Monday as we had expected to do because there was too much to do. The Bank, the Emigration Officer, the petrol coupons and then petrol, Post Office, shopping all took us the entire day in spite of the fact that we were driven round in Mr. Mackenzie's car. Wherever we go through all the official business of passports and carnet for the lorry to be looked into at every town, all taking up a great deal of time.

We left here on Tuesday morning on a very bad road and camped after 120 miles. The following morning we saw that we had broken 5 leaves of our front spring and the other spring was looking very tired. Dick and I decided to hitch-hike back to Kano to get new springs. We walked three miles back to a village to find out whether anything was going to Kano. They said lorries passed so we sat and waited from 9.30 to 2.00, we were just giving up and finished our last drop of water when one came. A lorry full of ground-nuts. I was put inside with the native driver and Dick sat on the ground-nuts with other natives having a lift. His was the better place as there was a faint breeze as we went along but I had none of that and the heat was terrific – over 100° in the shade. The driver stopped every half hour or so to cool off the engine and all the natives drank from the nearby rivers – very tantalising for us and I have never been so thirsty. We eventually arrived here at 11 pm, 120 miles taking 9 hours. We had difficulty finding a bed when we arrived but found both Guest Houses full. As we did not want to go back to the Mackenzies, we asked a stranger if there was anywhere else to stay – he said no but insisted that we spent the night with him. People are so kind.

The Mackenzies took us to see Kano City with its 14-mile-wall – we went up the mosque tower and looked down on the hundreds of mud houses and tiny enclosed yards containing the family and all their animals in about 10 sq yds – in comparison the vastness of the Emir's palace and grounds.

Evening
We have got our new springs and are taking them to the truck early in the morning so I hope they fit this time. Very much love. I only wish I could tell you more.

Beth

After various other breakdowns we arrived at Fort Lamy.* Crossing the river Chari was relatively hi-tech compared with the ferries we had to use in French Equatorial Africa, which consisted of boards put across dug-out canoes powered by Africans who sang as they paddled. We were relieved to reach the far side of these crocodile-infested rivers.

Maiduguri, British Nigeria 3 March, 1949

Darling Pa,
I don't know how long letters take to reach you so I am writing a short birthday letter to you now wishing you very many happy returns. I think of you all the time and realize how you would have enjoyed this trip. It is so full of interest and lovely unspoilt country, glorious sun and blue skies. We have had bad luck in Nigeria as first of all we had a petrol block, then the broken springs and after that the dynamo went and both batteries were too low to proceed at more than about three miles an hour. This was only fifty miles from where we'd stopped with broken springs. The springs we got made in Kano and got another lift back on a ground-nut lorry – a long, tedious journey over very bad road, but as we did not

---

* Now N'Djaména, the Capital of Chad.

leave Kano till 4:30 pm and arrived at the truck at 2:00 am (only 118 miles) we
at least were reasonably cool travelling during the evening. All the villages by the
wayside were lit up by large fires and the natives sitting round either cooking their
food or selling goods, it was all delightful.

Our driver stopped every hour or so either to see his pals or buy cigarettes
or a piece of fried fish on a stick that the natives were cooking on their fires. All
the natives seem awfully gay and always ready to help. When our batteries and
dynamo gave out we had to sit and wait for a truck to pass (we waited from
3:30 pm to 6 pm) and eventually persuaded the driver to swap batteries with us
temporarily. This was difficult to arrange as he did not understand English but
one of his passengers managed to interpret a little. We then proceeded here without
further delay.

We have managed to get a new armature for the dynamo and so are now
just about to press on to Fort Lamy and then to Bangassou and into the Congo.
Wherever we go in British Nigeria we are given the greatest welcome, and here in
Maiduguri we have been given a great deal of help. Dick and I were invited out to
dinner last night. The others have spent the last two nights at the rest house here.
Dick and I slept in the truck outside. The rest house is a roof with light and water
laid on and a boy to do our washing, which was black. He washed it and ironed it
all in five hours. We have all been invited out to breakfast so I must stop now. So
much love to you. Do try and see G and A before they leave in April.

Beth

We drove on through forests and villages. The people were curious and
friendly. Reporting to the local Commandant and handing him the briefcase with all the documents had become routine, but when we reached
Bangassou the officials announced that the Carnet de Passage for the
lorry was missing. At Fort Archambault★ 250 miles back it had not been
put back with the rest of the documents. There was not enough petrol to
go back. We were told it would take three weeks to have it sent by which
time the children were due to arrive in South Africa. At this point the man
whose jeep we had helped to rescue in the desert arrived and suggested
taking one of us on and that had to be me because Dick wanted to stay
with the lorry and still hoped to climb in the Ruwenzori and Mt Kenya.

★ Now Sarh in Chad.

Near Bangassou 9 March 1949

Dear Mother and Father,

Here we are on the borders of French Equatorial Africa and the Belgian Congo. We never seem to have a dull moment. Since we left Nigeria the country has changed a great deal again and now instead of parched dried-up look the countryside is beautiful fresh green with some very vivid flowers. Bananas, mangos are growing by the wayside and every village we go through the natives rush out waving and shouting. I adore the little black babies that go everywhere on their mothers' backs. The children of 3 and 4 years aren't so attractive as they have such huge protruding stomachs.

We were stopped in one village by some natives. They could not speak French or English but managed to make us understand there was a man in the village who had had a snake bite. We went to see him in his tiny hut full of people and a camp-fire and the snake, now dead, tied to a stick beside it. We cut round the wound with our snake bite pencil and put in permanganate. We then found that the nearest doctor was 40 miles back so we had to go that extra 80 miles to tell him. That for us was 6 hours. Recently we have been doing some night driving in order to cover the ground as we seem to have got along so slowly. However, in spite of driving all last night in order to get to Bangassou, today we find a bridge

Crossing a river without a bridge

E in village of man with snake bite

In same village, man holding lioncub

in the process of being mended. We cannot cross it until tomorrow night. That sort of thing happens a great deal.

At Fort Lamy we stayed the night in order to get some spare springs. We had two glorious bathes in a lovely sandy river called the Chari. We took our soap in with us of course. I even washed my hair and dived in several times to rinse it. Since then we have found several nice streams to lie in and wash in, but the rivers are now a bit risky.

Africa is a wonderful country. The country, the animals and birds that we've seen are beyond belief. I do wish I had books of African birds and flowers. I love the heat, it's so much easier for this sort of life, and so far we have only had half an hour of rain since we left, but I expect we may run into storms now. Think of us cooking over our camp-fire every night, the birds and crickets and jackals and other animals making so much noise we had to shout them down. We have cooked everything from a pigeon to a gazelle. Wild goose was exceedingly tough. Pigeons we had the most success with.

I wonder so much whether you are having some nice spring sunshine or icy March winds. I feel awfully spoilt having such a large helping of glorious weather. It will be a week or two yet before we get to Nairobi and I hear news of you which I long for.

My love to you both,
Beth

I was put in a difficult position when the decision was made for me to go with the man to Nairobi. There was no choice and I had to travel on sharing a tent with a strange man. We crossed the Bomu River to the Belgian Congo through rough thick jungle and violent rainstorms. The jeep had a hood but no side curtains – I was sitting in deep pools of water and the temperature dropped 20 degrees. After reaching Stanleyville,* we drove due east towards Uganda passing through the Ituri Forest where we saw the indigenous pygmies and were astonished how small they or rather how big we were in comparison. My travelling companion treated me with respect and consideration – I did not see him again after our parting in Uganda.

We carried on into Uganda. We passed the Ruwenzori Mountains which we had hoped to climb and after another twenty miles the jeep broke down. We had overtaken a local bus – there was no other traffic – and when it caught up with us the driver came to our assistance but without success. So I had to leave on my own and take the bus saying I would send a mechanic back to fix the jeep.

It was dark when we reached the next town, Mubende. Few people spoke English and no Europeans lived here. But by sign language I asked them to send back a mechanic and then asked for the DC thinking he would be happy to welcome someone from home. I eventually persuaded the bus driver and his friend to drive me the five miles to the DC's house. Here I got a cool reception – the DC himself in dinner jacket and black bow tie opened the door and seeing me in dirty shorts and flanked by two black men was horrified. He called his wife from her dinner to join him. She was in a long flowing evening dress. They really kept up appearances in the outposts of the British Empire. Eventually only I was invited in.

The servants were told to put on water so that I could bath (they saw the necessity) and I was given dinner and a bed for the night. The next morning they drove me to the bus going to Kampala. The bus, being full, had left ahead of time. The DC, complaining, drove fast to catch it. I was put in front, squashed in beside the driver and his girlfriend. The rest of the bus was full of people with their hens, ducks and goats. The DC's wife remarked: 'I've lived here twenty years and never been on one of these – I do hope you'll be all right.'

The bus engine was making awful noises; the driver left it running in neutral when every few miles he dropped into some hut for a drink, until

---

*   Now Kisangani in the Democratic Republic of Congo.

The Jeep by the river in Stanleyville

out in the bush it conked out completely. None of the occupants seemed surprised or put out. They took their belongings and settled under banana palms. One man took his new basket chair from the top of the bus for me to sit on. A couple who must have thought I was a missionary doctor came with suppurating sores for me to attend to. There was no traffic either way for three hours. I wished I had had my camera. At last there was an open lorry going towards Kampala. The bus driver and I stopped it asking for a lift. The driver looked at me enquiringly and then I was allowed to join the soldiers on the back. They all had their front teeth removed and wore pillbox hats. Smiling and friendly, they folded their coats for me to sit on and spent the journey entertaining me in sign language and showing me animals and vegetation of interest as we passed. We arrived at the bus station in Kampala where I phoned round hotels for a room for the night. All were full. One offered me a bed in a room with a French woman, without her permission. She was naturally displeased to find she had a room-mate.

I had booked a ticket on the weekly train to Nairobi but in the hotel that evening, I met someone who was flying to Nairobi. He said the trains would be hot and took so long, on his advice I flew arriving in Nairobi at 1 pm the next day. Awaiting me there were letters from home saying the children had measles and their passage had been delayed, so there was no rush after all.

Nairobi 24 March, 1949

Darling Mother and Father,

    Here I am in Kenya, but, alas, alone, as Dick and party got held up in Bangassou, French Equatorial Africa, and looked like being there for 2–3 weeks at least, so, when I was offered a lift with someone else coming this way, I had to take it. I was very sad indeed at leaving our party and the truck, which had been such a good home for so long. Well, I came on in this Jeep for 11 days, till it broke down 60 miles this side of Fort Portal. When after an hour and a half the native bus came along, I decided I must take that, and it landed me up, well after dark, in a native town where there were no white people, no hotel or rest house, no one speaking English. After a great deal of argument, which took over an hour, I eventually managed to persuade them to take me to the DC's house, which was 5 miles away. He and his wife were in the middle of dinner (evening dress and all). Large, smart house. I arrive, looking like a tramp with my luggage and three black boys in tow. They were obviously rather astonished, but could hardly refuse to give me a bed. They also gave me dinner and a bath (what a treat), and took me down to catch the native bus going on to Kampala, in the morning.

    This bus broke down 50 miles from Kampala. Everyone (all natives speaking Swahili, including the driver) just got out, taking it as a matter of course, and it seemed to me were quite prepared to spend the night there by the roadside. After 1½ hours a lorry full of Ugandan soldiers came along and I stopped them and said 'Kampala?' They nodded, so I got my luggage and climbed up on the open truck, with the soldiers all highly amused. These two days were almost the most exciting of the trip. I was treated with the utmost courtesy, and, in spite of no language, got on well with the natives of Uganda. At Kampala all the hotels were full, but I eventually managed to get a room, sharing with a French woman, and in the morning flew on here. Give me a native bus any day, in preference to a plane. I thought I was a good sailor, but I only just managed to hop from Kisumu here intact. That took one hour, and Entebbe to Kisumu one hour. We stopped for 20 minutes at Kisumu. I made friends on the plane with someone who said it was a particularly bumpy, unpleasant flight.

    I am staying here with friends of Sibyl's. They are most kind and hospitable. I have already been offered a lift to Jo'burg by car, and, if it is going soon enough, will take it, but I must get there very soon, as Miss Tasker is coming home and we want to try to buy her house, and she is ready to hand her pupils on to us. Our distinguished lawyer friends have written asking us to stay until we are settled in,

and Miss Tasker wants to give a party for us, and says many friends and neigh-
bours are waiting to help us! We really are very lucky.

Will you write to me c/o V. C. Berrangé, 5 Eden Road, Bramley, Jo'burg. They
will be a great help to us. They know we like Irene Tasker's house, and they think
that the goodwill, and not to mention the telephone which is an added attraction,
will be a great help to us. I hope Dick will be able to follow me fairly closely.

It was wonderful having all your letters, and Mama's and other news of Eng-
land. I'm afraid at times I feel very homesick. I'm longing to see the children. Pa
must see Adrian as well as G, if he can, as he sounds such a lad, and never walks
now but runs, and is furious if Margie catches him; this at 16 months sounds so
like our precious Julian, and it almost breaks my heart not to be with him. Stuart
says he will bring G. to see you at Easter; he sounds very grown up and friendly.

Mr Whitcombe has just said he can get me a passage to Durban on Monday,
so I expect I'll take that.

All love,
Beth

I decided to go by train to Mombasa and on to Lorenzo Marques, by
sea, a restful and interesting trip calling at Zanzibar, Dar-es-Salaam and
Beira on the way. It was on that trip I met an attractive young woman who
is now Lady Lasdun.

My introduction to South Africa was not pleasant. In the train from
Lorenzo Marques to Johannesburg police took me to an empty compart-
ment and searched and interrogated me. They thought I was up to no
good. I had no return ticket and little money. Fortunately I could give
Irene Tasker's name and address and they seemed satisfied. I could hardly
believe it when I arrived and was warmly greeted by her and Yolande Berrangé.

The house in Johannesburg bought from Irene Tasker

5   South Africa

Arriving at last and alone in Johannesburg after three months travelling, I was able to stay with good friends Yolande and Vernon Berrangé. I was overcome with the whole environment, their beautiful house, and garden full of flowers, the huge swimming pool and the endless South African sun. This seemed a haven after months of travel and at last I could take a long hot bath.

I met up with Irene Tasker and some of her pupils; we had planned to buy her house but I was a married woman and had no rights so I had to cable Dick to fly south before Irene left otherwise the contract could not be signed. The house was at 12 Cluny Road, Forest Town. Dick eventually arrived before Irene left and we bought and moved into her house before the children were due, so we were able to meet them together at Durban. It was good to be together again.

Irene Tasker

The family in 1949

House staff in 1949

The house was close to the zoo – one could hear the lions roaring, especially at night and it was the obvious place to which the children could be taken on their daily walk. There were jacarandas in the garden – their heavenly blue flowers were a delight on the tree and, when they dropped, formed a blue carpet for us to lie on. Climbing up the house was a bignonia cherere producing red bugle-like flowers most of the year. The climate was a joy for gardeners – one could grow sweet peas in winter and have a blaze of colour all year. We dug up some garden and built our own small pool to teach the boys to swim. They had a good healthy outdoor life.

We took over Biddy, Irene's dog, who understood the warning, 'Biddy, I'm teaching' – she would immediately go to her bed. We were also given another dog, a large poodle called Casse-cou, and a pure black cat, that Dick named Snowball, who became good friends. Among our livestock, we had a pair of bantams and later, fifty day-old chicks which in time produced plenty of eggs. We had the privilege of employing a delightful black male house servant called Joseph. He cared for us as though we were part of his own family. He introduced us to the market where we could buy large boxes of paw-paws and granadillas, guavas and avocado pears, all unusual but delicious. Sadly the South African police found that Joseph came from Rhodesia and sent him back for good.

Life seemed very different in South Africa with no ration books and with servants available. People had time to be sociable. However, very

Forest Town swimming pool

soon we were conscious of the serious political situation and many of our friends were in the anti-apartheid movement helping the black population to gain their rights. There was a lot of bad feeling between the Afrikaans and the British and black South Africans. It was embarrassing that white people had priority over the black people both in shops and public places. Black people had separate buses and schools and were treated as inferior, fit only to be servants of the white population. During the twelve years we lived in South Africa we were conscious of this unsatisfactory state of affairs although we took advantage of it and were able to have wonderful help from black people. Our children loved their nannies.

We were made to feel very welcome in South Africa, and soon had a large circle of friends from different backgrounds. When my father came to visit he was astonished to be introduced to so many people. We became friendly with Alan Paton after reading his book, *Cry the Beloved Country* (he later visited us in England). We also enjoyed the company of that great evangelist Trevor Huddleston who worked so hard for equal rights in South Africa.

After my mother died in 1949, my father came to visit us and went on to Victoria Falls, where he met Nora, an actress from the UK who later became his second wife. Back in England he had been living on his boat *Valerie*, but he then changed *Valerie* for a smaller boat called *Folksong* and bought a cottage on the Hamble River for them both, ideal for his sailing interests.

Having bought Irene's house, we also bought her teaching table. Two of our children were born on that table in the house in Forest Town. The night Richard was born the lights fused and I was impressed that the electricity department when I told them I was in the process of giving birth came and fixed them immediately.

In those days Europeans were expected to give birth lying down. Thanks to the Alexander Technique I had easy births, though the midwife made terrible faces because Richard had the cord around his neck. This had to be cut before he could be delivered. Speed here was imperative. Margie, who had looked after our sons on the voyage from England, was still with us at this time. When she left we employed black nannies who were instinctively good with babies and if they were in distress would sling them on their backs – this gave them great comfort.

The next baby born was Julia. After four boys, we were thrilled to have a daughter. Again she was born at home on the teaching table while Dick was teaching downstairs. Her birth was even more traumatic as, after a week, I haemorrhaged quite severely and had to be rushed to hospital where I was given a blood transfusion that sent me into rigours. It was a nasty experience caused by a bad blood match – so no more blood.

By the time Lucia was born we had moved to a smaller house and so she was born in hospital. I was allowed to get up almost immediately. Previously I'd been kept in bed for two weeks – the policy at that time. And now active births have become a sensible and more efficient practice.

Through the Berrangés we met lawyers and barristers who had helped FM and Irene to win the Jokl case – a libel case against the charge that the Alexander Technique was 'quackery'. They also introduced us to many men and women working for freedom against apartheid. In 1953, at a party of these supporters we met Nelson Mandela and talked to him for some time and came away appreciating that he was a very special man. He was a lawyer, obviously blessed with great strength and intelligence, but little did we know what he was to go through and what a great leader he was to become. We soon became aware of the huge racial problems . . . but we selfishly adjusted to living the privileged life of white people. We enjoyed teaching the Alexander Technique and many of our pupils became close friends. We had a varied and busy social life.

Our youngest son Richard particularly enjoyed visits to a friend's farm where he rode out with the manager. 'We were just like cowboys,' he said.

Nelson Mandela in his younger days

Dick's mother with Julia, and Richard, on the rockery Elisabeth created out of the hard tennis court at Westcliff Drive, Johannesburg

Richard, aged eight, riding a horse over jumps

He was a natural rider and later won horse trials and rode at the Barcelona Olympics.

We had many interesting pupils. One of Dick's pupils encouraged him to play golf again, and so after fifteen years of not playing he practised for a week or two. He then qualified for the South African Open Championship and happened to play with Gary Player who asked his advice at one stage. (Dick said his golf had improved since his AT training course.) We both played, and met many top golfers. Bobby Locke, surrounded by admirers, called to Dick in recognition as he modestly passed. Dick had played a demonstration round with him in the UK years earlier.

After post-war Britain South Africa was like a breath of fresh air. We had the opportunity to rock-climb with some top climbers in the Magaliesberg area (a range of rocky hills about thirty miles from Johannesburg) and in the Drakensberg – an Afrikaans word meaning Dragons Mountain. It was a joy to climb in 'tackies' as we called gym shoes, rather than heavy nailed boots. On one climbing trip a rock my foothold gave way and I fell and swung on the rope like a pendulum across the rock face. I was knocked unconscious which cut short that trip. I had a very painful ribcage for weeks afterwards. Among our climbing friends were the well known climbers, Harry Barker, and Schaff and Francesco Villa.

We had camping holidays by deserted beaches on the east coast as well as down near the Cape. One of these was at Isipingo (1949) where Dick went to practise golf before competing in the South African Open Tournament. Susan, whom I had met on the ship from Kenya to Lorenzo

The boys camping at Marina Beach

Susan Lasdun and the boys

Marques, came with us on this holiday. Later she married Denys Lasdun, the architect who designed the core buildings of East Anglia University and the National Theatre. We had our tent right on the beach but when the spring tide came up we had to move further away. This scared Mark who was two years old who kept saying, 'the sea's going to get me.'

Susan came on holiday with us the following year when Richard was still in a baby basket. That year we drove to Cape Town (about a thousand miles from Johannesburg) and camped in a wooded area near the settlement called Fish Hoek on Cape Point, the peninsula that separates the Atlantic and Indian oceans. It was wonderful swimming in the Indian Ocean. Once we visited a beach on the Atlantic side but the children refused to go into the icy waters.

We also had a holiday at Ramsgate, not far from Durban in Natal, where we shared a house on the beach with another family. We had been told to watch out for the extremely poisonous snakes that lived in the long grass. Our boys learned to watch where they put their feet and to make loud noises to keep the snakes away. The other family with whom we shared the house were always complaining about the racket the boys were making.

One of the best holidays we had in South Africa (1958) was at Umgazi Mouth in the Transkei on the east coast. (The Transkei was one of the areas designated by the South African government as home land for the indigenous South Africans.) Umgazi Mouth was the most dramatic estu-

One of my favourite places in South Africa: Umgazi Mouth in the Transkei

Family pictures at Umgazi Mouth

ary bounded by huge sand dunes on one side and rocky boundaries on the other. This time we stayed in small rondavels (thatched, round houses) on a grassy slope overlooking the sea. We had our simple meals in a large communal rondavel at the cliff edge. A local boatman would ferry us across the estuary to reach the steep sand dunes by the open sea. It was a wonderful area for children as they could paddle in paddle boats along the estuary or slide down the steep sand dunes and then cool off in the breakers of the warm sea. When Lucia who was one year old at the time got tired of making a beeline to the sea, Dick carried her in his rucksack. Just north of the rondavels we could walk into the native areas where we met some young men going through their initiation ceremonies with painted faces and traditional body attire. On another day, we drove to the nearby Petrified Forest – fossilized trees – and wondered how these had been formed. We felt that a more idyllic holiday situation would have been impossible to find.

As well as our climbing and seaside holidays, visits to the game reserves were a great treat. In the 1950s, these were informal. We sometimes camped or we stayed in rondavels with adjacent blocks of WCs and showers. In the open were large log fires on which to cook. One time we did not lock the cupboard by our rondavel and a cheeky hyena stole the cold bag containing food, eggs, bacon and tins of butter. It left a trail of its spoils (including an opened tin of butter) out of the camp. We were amazed that it had jaws strong enough to open the tin. We used to leave the camp at 6:00 am, unescorted, to look for big game, our cameras and binoculars at

Hyena

Zebras

Views of Kruger National Game Reserve

the ready (it is good to be early when the animals are moving before the heat of the day). One of the children with their eagle eye would be the first to spot a lioness and her cubs. We would quietly draw up at the side of the sandy track to watch them in action. It was scary when we were faced with a herd of elephants. They were not frightened of humans and have been known to crush a car. We switched off the engine and remained very quiet hoping they would find a tree to push down or something to hold their attention. The reserve was full of animals of all sizes and beautiful birds building their intricate hanging nests. There was always more and more to see in the game reserves. It is good for the African economy that they have attracted tourists from all over the world.

At one stage Dick supplemented our income working on a mushroom farm, cycling to and fro. On one occasion he fell and was knocked unconscious. Taken to hospital he was labelled 'unknown white male.' He had a fractured skull and a broken collar-bone. He was a hardy man and made a quick recovery.

In 1955 Dick, who had always been an explorer of many spiritual and psychological teachings in addition to that of Alexander, decided he must learn more about G. I. Gurdjieff and to do so we must move back to the UK. We had sold the house and most of our furniture when, by chance, Dick was introduced to an Indian guru. So there was a change of plan – we decided to stay on in Johannesburg. We house-hunted and eventually bought a newly-built one on an old hard tennis court. It was a challenge for me to make a good garden. It was hard going but thanks to a good climate the result was amazing.

Dick's mother visited us from the UK every two years. She was always wonderful with the children and a joy to have with us. Ever since Julian, who had difficulty with some words, called her Danny Jo, this nickname was used by the whole family.

In 1959, my father had suffered a heart attack in England and I wanted to see him and let him meet his grandchildren. Dick could not come with us. Air travel was quite expensive so I took our five children (Gavin, aged fifteen, Mark, aged eleven, Richard, aged eight, Julia, aged five, Lucia, aged two) by train and sea.

We started off by train to Cape Town. At one point, Richard, looking out of the window, got a live cinder in his eye and as a consequence was in pain the whole way. So on arrival in Cape Town we had to go to an eye specialist who fortunately was able to extract the object and relieve the pain. After that we spent a night in an hotel before boarding ship.

The sea trip, in a cabin in the bowels of the ship, was nightmarish, especially as the ship was short of water and oil and bobbed around like a cork. It was difficult to keep our food down. We had no porthole. On reaching the Canary Isles we refuelled and took on water so the voyage was slightly more comfortable. None of the children seemed to be perturbed. Mark had to look after the little ones at the children's meals. Gavin ate with me in the main dining-room. He was quite adventurous in trying the various dishes but he drew the line at smoked eel.

By the time we arrived in the Solent, there was a thick fog. The ship dropped anchor, unable to continue, we waited, and eventually were transported ashore in the ship's lifeboat. As we approached the dock, we were glad to see my father who had promised to meet us waving a red umbrella. Eventually, we took a train to London where my mother-in-law (Danny Jo) welcomed us all into her home in Kensington.

While we were there, my brother Stuart and his wife Joy came and took us on a guided tour of London. Later, Mark and Richard went by themselves by tube to St Paul's Cathedral, tried out the Whispering Gallery, and got lost on the way home. I worried but my mother-in-law was confident that they would find their way back.

On this trip, which was supposed to be partly educational, I was determined to take the boys with me to see more of Europe. My wonderful mother-in-law offered to look after the two girls with the help of a nanny.

Our trip to Europe had been thought out in Johannesburg where we had bought a Peugeot estate car and had arranged to take delivery in Paris, before letting the company ship it back to South Africa.

Without advance booking, I set off on the slow train to Paris with Gavin, Mark and Richard, equipped with a tent, sleeping bags, gas cylinder and billycans. Once it had crossed the Channel the slow train proved to be a big mistake – it stopped at every station. 'Are we there yet?' was the constant cry. At the Gare du Nord, we discovered that our tent and other luggage had been put on a fast train, so Gavin used all his initiative and sign language to seek it out. By good fortune it was discovered and we stuffed all our gear into a taxi. With a foam mattress protruding from the back we demanded, 'Bois de Boulogne, s'il vous plaît!' It was dark by this time. With bad grace, the taxi-driver dumped us at the campsite, demanded double the fare and departed. The boys pitched the tent and in a short time all four of us were snuggled up together, happy to be lying in the shelter of our tiny tent. It started to rain.

Next morning Gavin and I went in search of our new car, leaving eleven-year-old Mark in charge of Richard and the tent. We tried the metro but

Campsite at Bois de Boulogne in Paris

A pleasant view of Paris

it was on strike, so we took buses into central Paris. We arrived at the Peugeot showrooms at midday only to find them closed until 3:00 pm. Our only option was to have a sandwich and wait. But there was another problem: we had to negotiate the buying of the car and get to a bank to get petrol coupons before 4:00 pm. We arrived at 3:55, just in time. Then, how to drive this spanking new car, on a different side of the road, through the streets of Paris to the Bois de Boulogne? Luckily, Gavin has a great sense of direction. Glancing at the map he guided me round the Place de la Concorde, along the Champs Elysées indicating which lanes to move into so that we arrived safely at the Bois to find the two boys happily at home in the campsite. I think they had begged food from other campers who took pity on these deserted kids.

We had arranged, in advance, that the Peugeot was to have its first service at Annecy. On the way there we visited Chartres and Bourges with their wonderful cathedrals. In Annecy, we found a great site for our tent beside the lake. Miraculously, a telegram found us – it was addressed to: 'The Walkers, au bord du lac, Annecy.' It was from my sister-in-law Sibyl, who joined us there with her daughter Annie and they continued with us in our travels.

My aim was to see Rome. En route we drove over the Mont Cenis Pass into Italy where Mark and Richard experienced snow for the first time. We stopped at Porto Fino for all to swim in the Mediterranean. At Pisa, Mark and Richard went right up the tower. It looked very precarious from the ground with its dramatic lean. In those days you were allowed in all the ancient sites and buildings. Driving south we stopped in Perugia, Assisi and Spoleto. Tourists were few in 1959. In Assisi, Italian women sat outside embroidering clothes and I bought a child's dress for Lucia. On

Campsite at Annecy with Dick's niece, Anne Searight

First snow!

the edge of Assisi is the hermitage of St Francis. Inside it was quite cool and we were able to enjoy the wonderful frescos by Giotto undisturbed by crowds.

Rome was a great success. It was one of the few places where we had a guide to take us efficiently around all the places of great interest. The boys had lots of chances to run about and shake their legs up and down the Spanish Steps. I lost them in the Colosseum and a policeman found them climbing among the ruins of long-gone seats. We had the Sistine Chapel almost to ourselves so could lie on the floor to admire the frescoes on the vault by Michelangelo. From these feasts of art history we turned to drive back home.

On the way north, we visited Florence where we found even more to excite us. The campsite was near the Boboli Gardens overlooking the city and the Ponte Vecchio. The children loved the piazzas and at the Uffizi were overwhelmed by the paintings in the gallery. There was too much to enjoy and time was short as we wanted to visit Venice before leaving Italy. Camping outside Venice was spoiled by mosquitoes, but the canals, the gondola rides, St Mark's Square and the Doge's Palace made up for all the mosquito bites. The children's great joy was going in a gondola and Mark was even allowed to propel it. The glass-blowing at Murano was enthralling. Venice, with its treasures, bridges and narrow calles, was a haven for children to explore and we were loath to leave.

Our cultural trip was balanced by camping, sometimes in the countryside and then in the city. Everyone contributed with the chores: erecting the tent, packing the car, cooking and shopping. Not once did we have a meal out, preferring to shop at local markets. Our greatest problem was finding camping gas. On our way home, passing through Austria and Germany we camped in the Black Forest, then travelled back through France, passing Reims to see Joan of Arc on her charger.

On our return to England my father came up to Gilston Road to visit us all. Later I took Mark and Richard to stay with him by Southampton Water. At 6:30 the next morning Mark came to me and said, 'Richard's gone, and taken the oars.' My father's reaction was perfectly calm, unlike mine – I thought he might be washed out to sea. We found him happily rowing off the jetty in father's dinghy. We were then taken sailing in *Cena*, my father's boat, across the Solent to Lymington. Father patiently endured Richard's cry of 'Oooh! I wish we could go on that!' at every speedboat that passed. On another occasion, Gavin stayed with my father and went sailing with him. At one point on the trip down the Solent, my

Venice - Mark assisting the gondolier   *Richard in St Mark's Square*

Gavin is at the tiller, Elisabeth's father, Clive, looks unconcerned

father left Gavin steering and went below for a nap. A passing yachtsman took a photograph which, two years later, we were to see in a shop window in the West End of London.

In August we said tearful goodbyes to Danny Jo (Dick's mother) at the London docks as we boarded the *Edinburgh Castle*. Lucia's worst moment on that voyage was the 'crossing the line' ceremony when she was scared by people being pushed into the pool covered with shaving cream. We also won a prize in the fancy dress competition as 'The Old Woman who lived in a Shoe'.

On our arrival in Cape Town, Dick was there to meet us and we drove non-stop the 1,000 miles back to Johannesburg in the new Peugeot. In the middle of the night, a small deer bounded across the road but hesitated in our headlights – we were unable to avoid hitting it. We got out and found it had been killed on impact. We decided to take it home with us, where it was hung in the garage. Regretfully, our dog got to it before we could enjoy the venison. After our all-night drive, we needed to spend the next two days sleeping.

Hendrik Verwoerd, the architect of apartheid who was hated for his racist policies, was Prime Minister at this time and among Dick's Alexander pupils was a David Pratt. Pratt was attending the Rand Agricultural Show when during the show-jumping he tried, but failed, to shoot Verwoerd. Later Dick's friends jokingly complained that he had not taught Pratt a good hand-eye coordination. More seriously, it was probably the horror of the Sharpeville Massacre in March 1960 that prompted us to reconsider our lives and make the decision to leave South Africa. It was a big wrench and I would have hated to have missed my twelve years there. They really were an outstanding period in my life. Dick worked for the Congress of Democrats against the apartheid regime but close friends of ours were even more active in this area and spent much time in jail. Amongst these friends were the Slovos, the Bernsteins, the Fischers and the Hepners – all brave and dedicated people. Bram Fischer was on Robben Island with Nelson Mandela – I am honoured to have known these friends.

We were encouraged in our plans to move back to England by good friends and family connections. Mark's godfather, Anthony Furse, had offered to pay for Mark's education in England. Gavin had been advised by aptitude test consultants to train as an accountant and he decided, off his own bat, that he would go and do this in England. We therefore made plans to travel towards the end of December 1960. Gavin was to take his final school examinations in December so he stayed with our friends the Hepners and then flew to England after the examinations were over. He arrived in England before us and spent Christmas with Dick's uncle, Keith Freeman, and family.

6 Back Home

We returned to England by an Italian liner along the east coast of Africa. We came through the Red Sea and the Suez Canal. I managed to pay a visit to the remarkable museum in Cairo and see the Tutankhamun display and the pyramids; I also had the opportunity to ride a camel. We docked in Venice for four days so we had plenty of opportunity to see the sights although St Mark's Square was under water and we had to walk on duck-boards into St Mark's. We disembarked in Trieste. We drove the trusty Peugeot straight off the ship heading towards the mountains and snow to Igls in Austria, where we skied for two weeks before driving home.

On arrival in England we stayed in Kensington with Dick's mother, Danny Jo. She had made arrangements for the children's schooling, which was quite difficult for them, as it was all so different from the freedom they had had in South Africa. It was a problem settling with five children and their different needs.

During this time Dick's mother went to stay in Mull with her sister-in-law, Liz Freeman. She came home from this holiday feeling breathless

Family meal on board the ship bringing us home to Europe

and was admitted to hospital where she died. This was a great loss to the family as she was exceptionally loving to each one of us. She spread generosity to all.

—

Claud Phillimore was Dick's best friend at Winchester College and when we returned from South Africa we visited him and his wife Anne and son Francis and daughter Miranda at their beautiful house, Rymans, in the hamlet of Apuldram near Chichester.

On our first visit to the Phillimores, Francis was riding his new horse Pasha and Miranda was riding Mr Chips. They were exercising the horses around the paddock. Richard, aged ten, with envious eyes, said, 'Can I have a go?' He was offered a choice of horses and he chose Pasha. He looked very small on the horse's back but he confidently trotted round the paddock. Who was to know then, on that horse, he would win the Badminton horse trials in 1969?

Richard on Pasha doing dressage

Richard, show-jumping

HRH Queen Elizabeth presenting Richard (18) with the Badminton trophy in 1969

That first summer we stayed in the gardener's cottage at Rymans and Julia and Lucia went to school in Chichester.

The Phillimores became such close friends and were so welcoming that we spent many holidays and Christmas celebrations together. We camped in their duckery when there was no room in the house. We sailed with Anne in her Solent Sunbeam and raced with the Itchenor Yacht Club – often being reprimanded for our inefficiency, but it was great to be afloat on the Solent again after a break of twenty years.

Claud and Anne invited us each year to spend some time at Casteldardo, a large villa north of Venice in a wonderful situation at the foot of the Dolomites adjacent to the village Trichiana. Along its tree-lined drive you could look at beautiful views up and down the valley to the mountains. In part of this villa lived Juliana who loved to have Claud and his friends staying next door. She brought over marvellous Italian meals she had cooked (she showed me how she made her own pasta). She was full of fun and so hospitable that she invited us to stay in a special cottage at San Isidoro. This was an isolated, tranquil building with its own tiny chapel, with only the snow-capped mountains and the peasants scything the meadows as neighbours.

Villa Casteldardo

We would take our time travelling through France, Germany and Italy visiting special cities and places of great interest en route and by evening retreating to our tent. One year when we had Lucia with us, on our way there, we camped at Siena and San Gimignano where we met a friend from South Africa who was staying at a monastery in order to paint in the area. I remember one camp in a cornfield when we were woken by the sound of a galloping horse. It was Lucia running around the tent to warm up as she'd woken feeling cold. We also camped above Florence and went on to Ravenna with its beautiful mosaics but, unfortunately, there were swarms of mosquitoes at our campsite and we were badly bitten. We went on to the Jesolo campground just across the lagoon from Venice. From there we could go by boat into Venice. After all this camping it was quite a contrast to experience the luxuries of Villa Casteldardo.

From Casteldardo, there were many exciting walks down to the stream where we could paddle and cool our feet and listen to the water bubbling over the rocks, or we could climb up to Mount Pizzocco in the Dolomites and enjoy the variety and abundance of wild flowers on our way. We could go with Claud to see many old attractive towns in the area starting with the nearest, Trichiana, then Mel and on to the beautiful old town Feltre with its fifteenth-century buildings and piazzas all of artistic and archi-

Villa Casteldardo

tectural interest; specially appealing to my architect son-in-law who was with us.

The principal town is Belluno surrounded by mountains and in the valley of the rivers Ardo and Piave. The modern shops there contrasted with the remains of the ancient city walls and the tall elegant baroque Campanile. Then, at Asolo, we met Freya Stark, the intrepid traveller. We took her back with us to Casteldardo for lunch. She was an eccentric lady and entranced us enormously with stories of her many travels. In her seventies she went pony trekking in Nepal, saying she would sooner die there than anywhere else. She encouraged us to take some wonderful walks in the Dolomites.

Our next visit with Claud was to the Villa Foscari, called Malcontenta. The villa was built in the 1550s for the wealthy Foscari family and sits in splendid isolation beside the waters of the River Brenta. The Foscaris

Juliana and Freya Stark at Casteldardo

Claud Phillimore and Dick at Casteldardo

encouraged Andrea Palladio to bring his unique style to fruition so that it would reflect the importance of the family and its role in the history of Venice. The main facade holds the viewer in awe of its beauty and magnitude. The name derives from 'Malcontenti' in Italian, because in the old days thieves and robbers used to seek haven in the nearby marshes. Legend has it that one of the brothers banished his wife to live in the villa. I quote from Claud's own description of this villa, the day he first set eyes on it in 1933. He was travelling on a tram through the countryside near Venice with his stepmother:

> We gazed entranced.
> Suddenly rounding a long wide bend of the narrow tram track there came into view across a smooth lawn framed by tall poplars and weeping willows a gravely beautiful building. Worn and weathered, yet serene, with the colour of some warm old stone clothed with mosses and lichen, with a double flight of broad stone steps leading up to a lofty portico, it stood there bathed in the limpid autumn light. The impression was instantaneous, the impact immense. Round the next corner the tram lurched to a halt. Almost without a word of consultation or explanation exchanged we

Three views of Malcontenta

jumped out. The tram shook itself and went shrieking out of sight round the next bend like some fabulous monster, with a last flick of the tail. We were left with the silence and the sunlight. Hurrying back the few hundred yards we reached a point where we could gaze at the dream building across the canal. First impressions were only enhanced by finding its exact double reflected in the slow waters of the canal. There was no sign of life, but it was clearly inhabited. It seemed frustratingly unapproachable, though so near. And we knew we had to get there…We heard that the place had the rather haunting name of Malcontenta.

By this time we were under its spell and reckless of privacy and good manners. The gate was easily pushed open. We hid our picnic and our sketch books in a thicket behind one of the pillars, and walked on, trying to look respectable. There was no time to take in with more than a glance the very different and much more open and many windowed southern face of the villa, a great expanse of grass in front of it and flanking avenues of poplar trees, before we found ourselves ringing the bell beside a solid old door covered with round iron studs. After a time a window was opened cautiously above our heads, and then gently closed. There was an interval of several minutes before the door was opened by a manservant in a white jacket. We asked haltingly if it were by chance possible to visit the house and were told, yes. Long afterwards we learned that the owner had told the man to look out and tell him what kind of people were ringing the bell. Mercifully his report was apparently encouraging.

We confirmed his impression of the magical building. We were astonished at its beauty and grandeur. The owner, Bertie Landsberg, had bought it in 1924. It had suffererd from years of neglect and he had restored it with artistry and detail to its world-famous present state. On that first visit, Claud must have made a good impression and Bertie must have tuned in to Claud's delight and enthusiasm for his much-loved villa. Shortly after that first visit, Bertie went to his lawyer in Venice, and arranged to leave the villa to Claud, realising that he would want it to be kept up for many to appreciate in the years to come. When Bertie died in 1965 and his wife in 1973, Claud realised that he and his family could not take on the responsibility of looking after this world-renowned villa. He arranged to leave it to Tonci and Barbara Foscari who were architects and descendants of the original Foscaris, for whom the villa was built.

On our first visit we explored all the rooms admiring Palladio's cruciform plan giving such a sense of space and light. After lunching there we

Relaxing in the salone

Gondoliers arriving for their gala

had our siestas in the large salone lying on the couches below the frescoes on the walls and vaulted ceiling – all so luxurious.

Our next time at the Malcontenta was when the Venetian gondoliers came for their annual party. Decorated tables were spread out in front of the villa; the arrival on the canal of the gondoliers wearing blue and white striped tee shirts set the party going. After the meal there were sack races and other sports for the energetic. It was a great day.

The next week we had a day on the the island of Torcello which has a haunting history and so much on which to feast our eyes. We visited

Party for the Gondoliers

The Foscaris after the Gondoliers' Party

its atmospheric cathedral full of treasures from bygone days including wonderful eleventh-century mosaics and carved marble panels. At last, we dragged ourselves away and caught the boat to Murano where we watched the ease with which the glassblowers made such a variety of beautiful glass objects.

Anne Phillimore, who, before she married, was Anne Dorrien Smith, invited us to visit Tresco in the Scilly Isles where, coincidentally, my father had been stationed in the First World War and where he had met her family, then living at Tresco Abbey. Tresco is one of the most beautiful islands in the world with its internationally famous gardens. There were huge fields of daffodils. We had wonderful holidays there with Claud and Anne, visiting by boat inhabited and uninhabited islands in the area. During one visit the head gardener told us of the horrors of the huge storm when trees were blown down everywhere. He said the noise was deafening and there was no safe place to be. Visiting just after the storm we could see how trees had just missed an adjacent cottage by an inch.

When we arrived in London, Richard went to a school in Sloane Square which was very formal – the boys would file into classes and to lunch and

Storm damage to Tresco's beautiful gardens

Anne Phillimore painting a watercolour

One of Anne Phillimore's watercolours: Looking north from Rymans, West Sussex

on some days they filed into coaches and onto the sports ground, after games there was more filing back to the coaches. It was so different from South Africa where between classes they could chase each other around the kopje (hillside). He missed the freedom and exercise and became ill enough to have hospital investigations. Eventually we let him board at Highfield School, Hampshire, where he was able to excel at sports and swimming.

After spending some months in the Phillimores' cottage, we rented a house in Westleigh Avenue, Putney, for a year from friends who were leaving for Israel. They had an Afghan hound and asked us whether we would look after him while they were away. Dick knew that we would not be able to part with the dog after a year and said that he was only prepared to look after the dog if he was granted ownership. This was agreed and we owned a pet again. Dick used to exercise the dog by having him run to heel beside the bicycle that Dick was riding. The Afghan hound was beautiful and, as is the nature of his breed, always wanted to run away. We kept him until he died from a kind of leukaemia.

In 1962, the family with a friend of Richard's set off in the Peugeot on a ski trip in Europe, staying in youth hostels. The first night in Paris we slept in a large dormitory with three layers of bunks, not at all restful as the snoring and coughing came from all directions. Our main youth hostel was at Chateau d'Oex in Switzerland where there were two-storied sleeping shelves in each room; all the females slept on one shelf side by side and the males on an equivalent one. We found we were the only people who cleaned up in the kitchen. It was so cold when we left that the car wouldn't start and we were told to light a fire under the engine to warm it up. This we did with some trepidation, but it worked. The best youth hostel was one we had to ourselves at Les Diablerets, just like a private chalet. We collected the key, lit a wood fire, the heat from which went up to our sleeping area, all very cosy as it was snowing hard outside. In spite of the snow storm and lack of visibility, Lucia, then aged six, insisted that we all went out to ski on the deserted slopes, which was quite daring and magical. On the way back we nearly gassed ourselves in a hostel kitchen using the odourless gas stove to cook on. Luckily the warden came in and noticed.

Towards the end of our stay in Westleigh Avenue, we started looking for a house we could buy. We had renewed our friendship with the Gleadows who had a house at Redgrave Road in Putney. They helped us find a semi-detached house in Putney and we moved there in January 1963. Julia and Lucia went to the junior department of Putney Girls High. Later Julia went on to Godolphin and Latymer, which was her choice.

The family outside the Youth Hostel in Chateau d'Oex

*Youth Hostel at Diablerets: Top: Julia, Debbie Christie, Richard and Lucia
Below: Mark*

Family in Putney: Elisabeth, Gavin, Dick, Julia, Richard, Lucia and Mark

Au pairs provided child-minding so that we could both do some teaching. Dick and I both taught at the New College of Speech and Drama. He also taught at the Barlows' near the Albert Hall and I often went into the Carringtons' course where I continued to learn a lot from Walter's wisdom.

We found London claustrophobic after the wide open spaces in South Africa so with our friend Gerry Becker we spent time at weekends driving to Kent, Surrey and Oxford looking for our dream house. As we left these places the children would say, 'not quite what we're looking for.' On another such trip, Gerry made a comment that we all found most amusing: 'I love England; it is the only place in the world where fifty million eccentrics live in one place.'

We still had the Peugeot that I had picked up in Paris in 1959 and taken back to South Africa that year. We brought it back to Europe at the end of 1960 – it was a great vehicle and really proved its worth again taking six of us on skiing and camping holidays.

In 1967 we took Mark, Lucia and Julia with her friend Cathy in the Peugeot, all six of us, our tent, sleeping bags, food and gas cylinders (all but the kitchen sink) camping along the coast of Yugoslavia to Greece. There was just one complaint: the porridge had a faint flavour of petrol because the spare can had been too close to the food.

We rarely used campsites. Instead we found isolated, tucked-away spots where we could stay. Travelling along the Dalmatian coast was glorious. We stopped for a swim in the brilliant blue water followed by a picnic lunch then on to the fascinating town of Dubrovnik. It was then time to find a spot to camp for the night. We ended up spreading ourselves out amongst the Cypress trees at the end of a rich person's drive.

As we drove inland away from the coast we came to a deep gorge. We could not resist climbing down the rocks to the clear water below, stripping and plunging in. This sustained us for our drive into Greece and on to our next camping spot beside the Aegean Sea below Mt Olympus, which Dick intended to climb. We stayed a day or two before going on to the Sanctuary of Apollo at Delphi on Mount Parnassus – there was so much to explore amongst these ruins. We drove on to Athens and to the Acropolis and Parthenon where we could climb amongst the ruins. After this, we went to a Greek play. Leaving in the dark, we had to find a camping spot so we drove up a hill and parked unknowingly in a military

Swimming in the gorge en route to Greece

Lucia performing at Epidaurus

zone. In the morning, whilst we were having our porridge the military police arrived and wanted to arrest us. We calmed them down with sign language and a bit of ancient Greek. Immediately after breakfast, we left and went to Sounion and the temple of Poseidon, which was a great spot for our morning coffee. The next stop was Mycenae via Corinth on our way to Epidaurus. Here Lucia was able to demonstrate the acoustics of this extraordinary amphitheatre built in the fourth century BC and seating fourteen thousand people. Then we drove further south to Sparta and Mistras, the family tolerated all the driving by the fun we had camping and swimming in between. One of the best swimming spots we found was near Navarino, a place we called 'Spade Bay'; the sea was warm and clear and ultramarine. We camped there; we had our private beach, it was just wonderful.

Now it was time to head for home, and we drove to Patras where we took a boat to Brindisi calling at Corfu on the way. Now in Italy we went to Pompeii and on to Mount Vesuvius where the children were so embarrassed by Dick refusing adamantly to take a guide. Thus, under Dick's instruction, we climbed to its rim to look at the insides of this live volcano.

Holiday time was nearly over and we wended our way back through Italy via Florence and La Spezia, finding one or two special spots to camp and eventually crossing the Channel and back to London.

Setting up camp in Greece

On our next ski holiday we spent nights in a camper van. It was Easter when we first went to Les Deux Alpes where snow conditions were not good so we went on to Courchevel. We drove past a few grand houses and parked the van at the dead end of a road, a delightful spot. Our only company were the tiny field mice coming out of hibernation as the sun started to melt the high bank of snow. The sun also melted the frozen condensation in the van teaching us that when camping the following winter we should include an oil stove that would keep the inside of the van really warm. That time, in Ischgl, we parked behind a ski shop next to a cow barn. Our home-made jugged hare lasted several days kept in the snow beside the van but one day the snow was so frozen even the gas cylinder iced up and was unusable.

My first visit to the USA in 1969 was very exciting. Joan and Alex Murray invited me to East Lansing, Michigan, to teach some of Joan's students while she had her daughter. Alex taught the flute in the music faculty at Michigan State University. In the hospital they were most perturbed to find that Joan laughed during the delivery – from pleasure not distress. They thought she was hysterical.

It was my first time in America, and to be greeted on campus with 'Hi Elisabeth' made me feel immediately included. On our arrival there was

Camping in Courchevel – Lucia and Dick

snow and ice but this quickly changed to sunshine and the wonderful flowering dogwoods.

From there I went to Philadelphia and visited Professor Raymond Dart at the Institute for the Achievement of Human Potential. (He and his family were among our friends in Johannesburg.) I met his colleagues Glen Doman and Carl H. Delacato and heard about the interesting work they were doing with people with neurological problems. Dart demonstrated some of his interest in what is now called the Dart Procedures (developmental phases of child growth). His wife seemed concerned at his rolling around on the floor at his age.

The South African friends we stayed with showed me the highlights of Philadelphia including the famous art collection in the home of Dr Albert C. Barnes. The gardens all round were at this time ablaze with azaleas, dogwoods and all the beauties of spring.

Also in 1969, with Julia, Lucia and Mandy our cat in our camper van we had a holiday in Scotland. We spent two nights on the Isle of Skye where Mandy spent her time chasing field mice – she actually caught one which surprised us because it was the only time in her life when she managed to do that. We had the place we stayed in totally to ourselves.

It had been thirty-two years since we were last in Cruden Bay so we decided to return. The golf course and sea views were as beautiful as ever but the hotel and Dick's caravan were no longer there. The RAF had taken

In Skye with our cat, Mandy, Dick, Lucia and Julia

over the hotel during the war and it had become too expensive to repair the damages. We played a round of golf on the nine hole course which is inside the competition eighteen hole course. We drove the van into the small fishing port of Cruden Bay and there we spent the night. In the morning we watched the fishermen returning from sea, unloading a large catch of salmon among the other smaller fish. After breakfast we walked

Golf course at Cruden Bay

Fishing boat going out at Cruden Bay

round to the Bullers of Buchan. There we watched the bird life especially the peregrine falcon. It was exciting to be back at Cruden Bay again.

In 1970, looking in *Country Life*, I saw a picture of a house on the Thames. It was a William and Mary house built for the Preston Crowmarsh Mill owner around 1690. It was to be auctioned (it belonged to Tom Stoppard although he did not live in it). I bid at the auction and bought it, but worried madly afterwards, not knowing whether we could afford it. It was called the Old Mill House. From there we could commute quite easily to London and Lucia could go to school in Oxford. It proved to be a happy home for thirteen years. It was a beautiful house and had a good deal of space. The grounds included a big garden at the back and at the front, across the road, a water meadow next to a mill-tail on the Thames which often flooded in winter. Near the road, on a raised area in the water meadows, there was a swimming pool. We were able to keep poultry again. The bantams were a great joy to the family, especially Fred and Flo who produced delightful baby chicks. The parents roosted in the topiary with their heads just poking out the top, reminding me of the partridge in a pear tree. Surprisingly, a pair of swans proudly brought their cygnets to our front lawn. Their nest was on an island at the end of our grass and as soon as the babies hatched, they climbed onto their mother's back as she swam up to us.

The first big party at the Old Mill House was Richard's twenty-first birthday and then in 1974, Julia's twenty-first, when to Dick's and my

amusement we saw a few of the guests streaking into the swimming pool.
The following year Julia and Chris celebrated their wedding there. At each

Front and back views of Old Mill House, Preston Crowmarsh

Swans in front of the Old Mill House

of these events, we hired a rustic marquee that we decorated with ivy, trailing plants and streamers. We did all the catering, preparing weeks ahead so that with the minimum of expense we could give our family and friends a celebration.

Although this was in the country, people came from Oxford, Reading and London to have Alexander lessons with us. Among those who came to have lessons were the ethologist, Nikolaas (Niko) Tinbergen, and his wife Lies. Their daughter Janet, a cellist and Alexander Technique enthusiast, suggested that Niko and Lies should have some lessons. When Niko won a shared Nobel Prize for Physiology or Medicine in 1973, he spoke about the Alexander principles in his acceptance speech.* Niko continued to have lessons for another nine years, finding it of use for a time to relieve depression, from which he had suffered for some time. In 1980 we stayed with them in their idyllic holiday cottage, called 'Slakes' near Dufton in Westmorland. From there, Niko took us to Ravenglass where he had studied the seagulls. It was a special place for him and his friend Jimmy Rose – they were like a couple of schoolboys in their enthusiasm. It was a home

---

*   'Ethology and Stress Diseases' – Nobel Prize Lecture, 12 December 1973, by Nikolaas Tinbergen.

Dick and Kes with Niko Tinbergen at Slakes

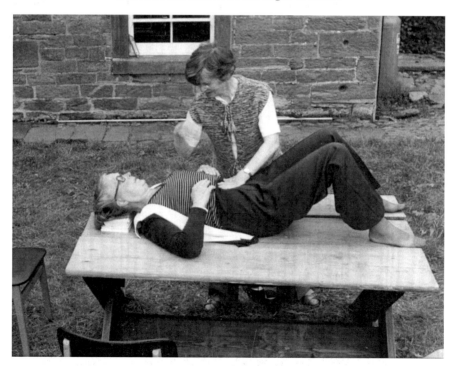

Lies Tinbergen having a lesson on the table

from home. Niko was also a keen photographer and he and I exchanged many photos.

In 1974 we went camping in Turkey. This was another great trip – we were then in our camper van – through France to Villach, Ljubijana, Zagreb, Belgrade, Sofia and on to Istanbul. I was horrified by the dangerous drivers in Turkey. The sides of the roads were littered with discarded cars. However, Istanbul had so much to offer. We brazenly parked outside Topkapi Palace and spent a day enjoying the wonders inside, including the Sultan's Harem salons. There was much to explore in the city: the Byzantine monuments and mosaics, St Sofia and the Ottoman monuments and the famous Blue Mosque – all too much to see in our restricted schedule. Many interesting places were on our short list: Denizli, Ephesus and Kusadasi. Amongst the white rocks in Pamukkale we bartered for some beautiful rugs, which we still treasure today. The van broke down in Denizli. We were lucky to find a helpful German mechanic who agreed to fix the van in the day-time, because we needed it to sleep in. Everywhere in Turkey we received such friendship and consideration.

Camping in Turkey was particularly good and in spite of other advice we found spectacular places to spend the nights, and never in a campsite. One day looking round an archaeological site we talked to a young Turkish man who invited us to what we thought was his wedding that evening. It turned out to be a circumcision party not a wedding but it was not to be missed. It took place in a very simple home enclosed by a white wall out-

Debbie Christie and Lucia wakened by the sun on the Marmaris Peninsula

Circumcision party

side which was a Mercedes Benz with a German number plate. The owner worked in Germany and so our German helped us to communicate. There was a band and dancing. Dick and I had to dance with the grandparents and Lucia and Debbie danced with the teenagers. This went on all night. We were invited to put our van into the next door enclosure where there were cows chewing the cud all night. In the morning we were woken with bowls full of milk, hot from the cow. The hospitality we received was so warm that I wish I could return.

We enjoyed the peninsulas of Marmaris and Bodrum. From the road you could see the sea on both sides. At the tip of one was a wonderful spot for the night. Continuing north along the coast, we came to Izmir and eventually to Troy, where the girls made friends with two fishermen, who invited them to go fishing. Suddenly we realised time was running out and we had to return home. Oh, what a lot of happiness there is to remember.

After our children left home, Dick and I continued to enjoy camping holidays and exploring different countries. We focused our visits on particular interests and one of these was Romanesque churches. We had at this time a two-berth camper van, which made it convenient to stop at a place of our choice for the night or for a meal. We usually crossed the Channel to Le Havre, arriving in France at 7:00 am. Always excited to

A meal with fishermen

be on French soil again with its cultural differences, we stopped at a village near Tankerville to buy freshly-baked baguettes and a quick breakfast, then drove non-stop along the A6 to Vézelay.

At the back of this abbey was the ideal spot to refresh ourselves with the picnic lunch before entering in awe through the majestic carved tympanum. Looking through at the architecture of the interior, we remembered Kenneth Clark's words, 'I can think of no other Romanesque interior that has this quality of lightness, this feeling of divine reason.' We allowed it all to enter our souls. We could spend days enjoying the amazing works of art, architecture and sculpture here, but we absorbed the twelfth-century atmosphere of these dramatic sculptures and moved on towards our next stop: the cathedral of St Lazare at Autun.

That cathedral was amazing for the work of Gislebertis. The tympanum is a great masterpiece and depicts the last judgement of grimacing devils, damned souls and trumpeting angels. In the chapter house hang his treasured carvings, now removed from the capitals on pillars of the nave, depicting biblical stories including the adoration of the Magi and the suicide of Judas.

From twelfth-century culture we moved to our campsite on the Rhône at Tournon. Here we met my brother and sister-in-law who were also enjoying this well-run site in the town centre, where we were able to stock up on fresh fruit and vegetables. Our next visit was to the pious city of Le

Typical carvings in Romanesque churches

Puy. Here we took our time in climbing up the sprawling 268 steps to the twelfth-century Chapelle St Michel with its trefoil-arch portal and minaret bell tower. Making a slow descent, we aimed for the cathedral, one of the great pilgrimage churches of medieval France – its dazzling coloured stone exterior rises from the side of a steep hill. We enjoyed the cloisters and the masonry of its arches, the carving of the capitals and the frescos within, as well as the lace-work motifs in the wrought-iron gate. Walking back, our interests were diverted by the traditional lace makers sitting by their doors – their craft dates back to the eleventh century.

We headed for the Puy-de-Dôme and volcanic national park. On the way we visited St Austremoine's twelfth-century abbey at Issoire, the largest Romanesque church in the Auvergne. We admired the geometric cone-shaped roofs and semicircular blind arches around the windows. There had been much restoration, but we managed to see the carving showing the Last Supper with Jesus and twelve disciples encircling a pillar.

It is fascinating to compare the artistry of all this Romanesque work and we moved on to the village of St Nectaire. The monumental church there is dedicated to the evangelist of that name who preached Christianity in pagan Auvergne in the fourth century. Among treasures here we saw the gilded bust of St Baudime. Still hungry to see more, we drove to the village of Orcival in its green valley in the foothills of Monts-Dore. Here stood the basilica of Notre-Dame D'Orcival, built of grey volcanic stone. The tiered domes of its characteristic chapel and its harmonious lines were a joy to the eye. The inside treasure is the enthroned twelfth-century gilded statue of the Virgin and Child, behind the high altar.

After these cultural feasts it was good to retreat to a camp beside the volcanic waters of Lake Chambon – a great place to recharge our batteries.

Our next campsite was in the town of Clermont-Ferrand, a well-kept municipal site with good hot showers. In the town we made a quick stop to see the eleventh-century basilica of Notre-Dame du Port, to admire the interior and simplicity of the naves and arcades as well as its sculpture capitals.

We loved the Auvergne and the Massif Central and the shapes of the extinct volcanoes. On our way home we camped at Aubusson, its shops full of old and new tapestries. There was so much to discover but, regretfully, we needed to return home to continue our teaching until our next trip.

Basilica of Notre-Dame D'Orcival

As the Old Mill House had become too big for Dick and I, we sold it to my nephew Christopher Clarke and searched the villages for another 'dream home' in the area. But, not finding anything suitable, we eventually decided that it would be better for us and our pupils to be in Oxford. We were lucky to find a house in central north Oxford, at 63 Chalfont Road, that needed upgrading. So we were able to almost gut the house and adapt it to our needs. The garden had been neglected so we had plenty of opportunity to create a colourful garden. We planted trees and shrubs and our favourite roses and several varieties of clematis. On the patio which we had built we had many pots of tulips and daffodils in the spring and geraniums and busy lizzies in the summer, not forgetting the sweet peas which were so lovely to bring into the house.

In 1983 Dick and I returned to South Africa for a holiday, and stayed with our very close friends Bill and Miriam Hepner. They met us at the airport and the gap of twenty-three years melted away. It was like returning home. Our love of these friends and love of South Africa was overwhelming. We renewed friendships and contacts with past pupils asking for Alexander lessons, with almost daily invitations to lunch, tea or dinner. On the first evening we went to a party to meet Phillip Tobias who in 1958 had become head of the Anatomy Department at Witwatersrand Univer-

Elisabeth's garden at Chalfont Road, Oxford

sity, Johannesburg, on the retirement of Raymond Dart who had held that post for thirty-five years. For eighteen of those years Dart was also Dean of the medical faculty. He and his family had Alexander lessons with Irene Tasker. Dart had a high opinion of Alexander's work and paid tribute to him in his FM Alexander memorial lecture on 20 March 1970, a most stimulating and inspiring talk★.

At the party Phillip Tobias gave a brilliant speech about his work on palaeo-anthropology and spoke of Dart as a most unforgettable character. We met there many other stimulating, intelligent and interesting people who seemed happy to talk to us about our life in England and their relations or friends who were in England, the apartheid situation had driven so many away.

Bill took us to visit the new Afrikaans College which had been built in Johannesburg since we had left in 1960. We celebrated Christmas Day with Helen Joseph, a political activist under house arrest. She had up to thirty guests, all ANC activists; there was a wonderfully warm and inviting

Africans in traditional dress

★ See Raymond Dart 'An Anatomist's Tribute to FM Alexander' in *Skill &
   Poise: A selection from the writings of Raymond Dart* (1893–1988), pp. 91–121.

atmosphere, one of a bond of friendship with people committed to fighting for human rights in South Africa.

Dorothy Morrison, who trained as an Alexander teacher with FM Alexander, was now doing her own version of the Technique. She had turned the shell of the very plain house we helped her choose twenty-three years ago, into an Italian villa. Her architect husband had helped to initiate this.

Miriam lent us her car so we were able to visit Jeremy Taylor, a well-known singer-songwriter in South Africa, and his present wife in their house by the Vaal Dam. We then drove to the Magaliesberg where we had climbed back in the fifties. This time we chose an easy climb with Bob Davis but now there were lots of modern climbing safety measures using helmets and also a clever device for putting in cracks of various size. It was

Our friends' Italianate 'Villa D'Este' in Johannesburg

Lucia swimming in Hout Bay

all very cumbersome compared with climbing in the 1950s wearing tack-ies on our feet and carrying no heavy equipment.

Some of our friends were members of a liberal group who wore a black sash showing that they believed and worked for racial equality and free-dom of the individual. A leading figure was Helen Suzman. In Johan-nesburg we sat in at a 'Black Sash' meeting to listen to Beulah Rollick's handling of problems with almost virtuoso brilliance knowing most of the relevant regulations and how to use them, and being able to help black Africans with their problems of inequality. At that same meeting Sheenah Duncan showed the value of the 'Black Sash' helpers, and how difficulties could be tackled without being imprisoned in South Africa.

We felt at home in this wonderful country with the sun, the paw paws and the boxes of granadillas. When the time came we were very sad to leave.

In Oxford we had many new pupils as we were accessible by foot, cycle or car and even the bus stopped at the end of the road. We were still able to commute to teach at the New College of Speech and Drama (the famous ballerina, Pavlova, once lived there). This had a big garden and was a nice venue for spreading the work. After teaching at the New College, we would teach pupils in their homes. Two delightful people, Jo and Winnie Hodgkinson, after their lesson would give us a tasty lunch including a glass of German white wine.

Hodgkinsons' cottage, 'Fornside', St John's in the Vale

St John's Beck, a short stroll from Fornside

In 1983 the Hodgkinsons insisted we should take a holiday in their cottage in the Lake District. The cottage, called Fornside, was in a beautiful position protected by a steep hill at the back, nestled on the lower slopes of Helvellyn. The walled garden was ablaze with roses, irises and clumps of cranesbill. We had a choice of many wonderful walks, mountains to climb and lakes to discover. Our first walk was along the stream to visit the church in St John's Vale in its delightful setting. Then we went to Wythburn and walked to High Raise where the views all round were spectacular. On the way up we spotted three very black baby minks and their mother darting in and out of the rocks. I am told that they are destructive to our indigenous wildlife, but I found them so attractive.

The following day we took the car to Grasmere and walked up the Langdale valley towards Skelwith and on to the summit of Pike-o-Blisco from where there was a clear view of the Langdales and the mountains and valleys elegantly shaped around.

On another day, we motored to Keswick. We walked from the Honiston Pass overlooking quarries of greenish slate and headed for Great Gable. We reached the summit via the west ridge, meeting other climbers on the top. It had taken us three hours steady going up and two hours going down. My feet were very sore from being on loose rocky and stony ground and from somewhat unsuitable footwear. The next day was beautifully

Dick in Langdale

clear and sunny and we aimed to climb Helvellyn from the Wythburn car park. The first thousand feet were very steep and then a more gradual gradient for the next 2,000 feet. There we found a spring and our little Jack Russell terrier, Kes, could stop panting. There was a slight breeze but the going was still hot. We reached Striding Edge and views of gentle ridges and buttresses sweeping in curves with lakes in the valleys and tarns in the fields. No wonder the Lake District is renowned for its beauty.

At Chalfont Road in 1985 Lucia and her dance group ('Joint Work') persuaded us to start our training course, the Alexander Teacher Training Course Oxford (ATTCO). In Oxford we made new and treasured friends who opened up connections with the colleges and their traditions. Jean Lodge, an artist who specialised in print-making and a Fellow of New College, took me to wonderful banquets at New College with its remarkable choir.

In 1985, our pleasure in camping and discovering beautiful unspoilt areas led us to visit Collioure, south of Perpignan in France, a delightful small fishing village dating back to the seventh century. It has attracted many artists including Picasso, Matisse and Braque. The amazing light and picturesque views of the castle and tiny harbour must have attracted them, Unusually for us, we went to a quiet campsite on the cliff overlooking a small sandy beach from which we could walk round the cliff

Our first training course at Chalfont Road

point into Collioure village. During our walk we watched the local boys diving from the rocks into the sea below. Collioure beach was unspoiled by crowds. The narrow streets and red tiled roofs of the small terraced houses, clustered around the bay, added to the special atmosphere. We could walk back to our campsite through dry grassy fields and over the hill and then cool off in the sea on the beach below. On a day's outing to Elne, a few kilometres inland, we spent time at the eleventh-century cathedral which was up a steep hill above the town, with spectacular views over the surrounding countryside and out to the Pyrenees. We took time examining the variety of beautiful stone carvings in the cloisters of the cathedral.

Back at our campsite, we were running out of time so we drove north along the Mediterranean coast past Sete, the large fishing port, and on to La Grande Motte, an extraordinary modern town designed in 1967. The town appeared to be made up of white blocks of apartments with no gardens, just streets dividing the buildings. We could see no shops or cafés; we found it difficult to find a place to stop and eat our lunch. Eventually we did manage to go along a street and see the sea. We parked illegally to eat our lunch in the car.

We were now heading for the Cévennes and had to drive along a very windy road to Florac near the Parc Nationale des Cévennes. En route we

Collioure

Dick admiring a gorge in the Cevennes

found a beautiful campsite and cold stream in which to swim. We were hurrying now and drove past Bourges and camped at a site in the middle of Clermont-Ferrand. This was a municipal site, beautifully kept with really hot showers and clean WCs. It certainly won Dick over to campsites as opposed to sleeping rough.

In 1987, with Lucia and her patner, Sharyn, we decided to explore Crete. We took cheap flights to Heraklion arriving there at 5:00 am. From there we took a taxi to Hania, a hair-raising drive. The driver swerved round corners at high speed in spite of my request to slow down but we eventually arrived safely at the old city where we sat on a bench and ate our home-prepared sandwiches waiting for the local inhabitants to wake up before searching for rooms to rent. Lucia and Sharyn eventually returned jubilant. They had found two rooms above a small rug weaver's shop in one of the delightful Venetian alleys near the old harbour. The landlady wove her own colourful rugs, she was friendly and helpful and we bought one of them. There was so much to see and enjoy as we sat by the harbour outside rows of small shops with people strolling by or riding in their horse and trap. We walked around the harbour to the old lighthouse seeing

Dick in Samaria gorge   *Lucia at Knossos*

the sea on one side, mountains in the distance and attractive old houses with their red roofs below. It was difficult to leave this delightful city but we wanted to visit Loutro, a small fishing village reached by small boat or an hour's walk along the seashore. We chose the boat and were rewarded by a most inviting view as we chugged slowly into the small bay, which was surrounded by white painted taverns, with bouganvillia draped from their rooftops, nestling at the foot of scrub and tree-covered hills.

On landing we asked at a café for rooms and we were fortunate to be told of one with a small kitchen and shower and an almond tree shading its patio, looking over the blue transparent sea. We could swim across the bay or walk in many directions. We walked up the hill above the bay to a small village, a strenuous walk on a hot day, but we were rewarded by a welcome from two of the few inhabitants, who gave us refreshing drinks and sweetmeats, refusing payments: they were so happy to receive visitors.

Walking down we enjoyed the aroma of the thyme, marjoram and other herbs as we crushed them with our feet, what a special place to walk. One day we took the boat onto the next village Agia Roumeli from where we could start to walk up the famous Samaria gorge. We did not go all the way up as it is a steep climb rising 800 metres, the top being close to the

On Crete a goat keeps watch

Harnia at Omalos. This gorge has been a refuge on the island during many wars, it provides a dramatic walk over a stream and between cliffs often merely three metres apart.

Before returning to England we took the bus to Knossos to see the remains of King Minos' Menoan palace. The painted walls remain still very vivid and the many magnificently designed five feet urns still stand beautifully restored. The whole setting reminded me of Greek mythology I had learned at school.

In 1988, we stayed in the house of Sarah and her husband Julian Lush at Burges, west of Foix in the south of France. It was so wonderfully situated for walking in the hills with views of snow-capped mountains and the opportunities it afforded to visit many places of interest as well as Foix, its castle and busy market, selling local produce.

In 1989 the Northern Open golf championship was held at Cruden Bay. In the 1930s Dick had won this championship twice, being eight strokes ahead of the next competitor, so was given a special invitation as a VIP guest. Returning to this special place and remembering again our

A short walk from the cottage west of Foix

first meeting, we enjoyed walking around this demanding links course, all very familiar. This time we stayed with a friend we had met in 1937, who was living in one of the chalets built on the site of the demolished hotel. It was good to renew her welcoming friendship.

After being photographed with the winner and sipping champagne with him, we drove back to Aberdeen and on to the Murtle Estate, the previous home of Dick's Freeman grandfather, all familiar to Dick as he had stayed there often. It is now a Steiner Camp Hill home. We were welcomed there like long-lost friends and shown round, Dick enjoying his memories in this large house that had not been altered but with small houses built in the grounds for the Camp Hill children. The original walled garden was still productive.

The next Scottish tour was to visit Elizabeth Freeman, Dick's uncle Wilfrid's widow, on the Isle of Mull. She had a secluded cottage overlooking a loch in an idyllic spot, 'far from the madding crowd.' We went over to Iona where we spent a day walking and picnicking on the rocks on the west side enjoying the March sunshine. Returning to the Abbey to the spiritual home of the Iona community, one felt a long way from the hurly-burly of our life.

Leaving Mull we drove on to Duntrune Castle standing high overlooking Loch Crinan. Dick's cousin and family were living here, in what I believe to be the only castle to have been privately owned and lived in

Murtle House, Bieldside

View of Mull from the house of Liz Freeman

since it was built. They had had a visit by boat from the Duke of Edinburgh and his entourage.

Duntrune Castle

I have been to and given workshops at five Alexander congresses. I have got so much out of each individual congress: they have all given me so much enjoyment, interest, and experience, and I really learned a lot from each one.

The Congress at Sussex University in 1988 was a good venue for people from all over the world to meet as the accommodation, meals, workshops and talks were all on campus. Groups from different schools shared work on the lawns in the open air and we observed their different approaches to the Technique. As we lined up in the self-service restaurant, we met and palled up with people from many varied backgrounds and Alexander heritages.

When Dick and I heard that the next Alexander Congress was to be in Engelberg, we decided to take a holiday there the year before. We had our small camper van and took the opportunity to camp through France and into Switzerland and to visit places in France on our way there and back, between walking in the mountains in Engelberg. During our meals beside the stream we watched the hang gliders descending from the mountain tops looking like butterflies and sometimes descending into the wrong area. This holiday gave Dick a taste for returning there the following year to the Congress. It was an ideal campsite with the snow-capped moun-

Above Engelberg campsite; Below: Hangliders at Engelberg

tains around and a grassy site beside a cool glacier stream which was good for cooling our bottles of beer.

Returning there for the Congress we hired the last two bicycles in Engelberg in order to cycle to the workshops and talks and back. Giving Adam and Rosemary Nott supper in the camper van one evening there was a tremendous thunderstorm and water poured down the mountains filling the stream so that we were worried that we would be washed away. Thankfully the rain stopped in time. Dick and I cycled into the centre to attend groups, classes, workshops, and dances. Most of the other teachers were staying in smart hotels. It was at this Congress that David Garlick invited us to the 1994 Congress in Sidney. Michael Frederick encouraged me to do some work with Bruce Fertman whom I met there for the first time. Dick and I assisted Marjory Barlow and taught some of the participants during her workshop. Bruce and I made a date which he promptly 'cut' in order to mountain walk (very sensible). We did not meet properly until Sydney where we worked together and he invited Lucia and me to Philadelphia to teach at his school in 1995.

On one of the coldest mornings on 14 December 1991 Dick went off on his bicycle with a dog on the lead, skidded on an icy patch, fell and broke his hip. That day there were queues of patients with broken bones at the hospital and he had to wait for a day to have a pin put in his hip. He came out of hospital two days after Christmas. But after two weeks at home he developed breathing problems and had to go back to hospital on 13 January 1992 where he died three days later. This was a great shock to us all as he had been in such good health.

Life is not the same without Dick. Of course life is never the same: changing minute by minute, but a huge part of me came to life as soon as I met Dick and in spite of difficult times together, our strong love survived and our souls were one. That inner strength has buoyed me up in these past sixteen years on my own. The Alexander Technique, my family and friends, have all been enormous supports, but life with Dick taught me so much and his spirit is still with me.

Dick never wanted people to mourn him and insisted that we should have a party rather than a funeral. We arranged a sit-down lunch at Benson village hall for seventy friends and family. It was a beautiful occasion when each one of his children paid tribute to their father in their own way, and other friends, students and colleagues spoke of amusing times they had shared with him. Musicians played and sang. It was a day to remember. A wonderful memory for me are the words of Gerry Becker as he left the memorial ceremony, he said: 'Elisabeth you were good for Dick.' I never felt I was good enough.

Dick was an unusual man, serious about life and searching for its meaning. His investigations included Christianity, Scientology, Gurdjieff, Hinduism and finally Buddhism which fitted well with Alexander's teaching. He also had many hobbies: mountaineering, sailing, and golf. He loved to travel, for him there was so much to discover, so much more to learn about the world and life. He often regretted that he didn't spend enough time mountaineering, or sailing or reading philosophical works or current writings, as well as teaching the Alexander Technique and meditating and enjoying his family. There wasn't enough time and of this he complained.

When Dick died my emotions were paralysed: part of me died, I could not cry, I was stunned, I could not believe that we had been separated. We had been part of one another for fifty-seven years, loving, teaching, climbing, travelling and learning together. How could just half of me continue alone? But thanks to the children he had given me, their love and support, and Alexander's teaching which helps one to be in the present and to handle each moment, I found I was able to carry on. I had much to do on my own.

I still had many students and pupils needing lessons and I knew it was Dick's wish that I should continue spreading the gift that FM had given us. My daughter Lucia and Bridget Belgrave were towers of strength in helping me to continue the training course. But oh how I yearn for the lost hugs, kisses and warmth of that closeness.

Then when Lucia and I were invited to give workshops at the 1994 Sydney Alexander Technique Congress in Australia it gave me confidence that I could teach without Dick's support. After Sydney, Lucia and I travelled all over the world teaching at training courses and workshops. I have now taught in fifteen different countries.

I hope we all stick to FM's principles as there is no doubt that he taught and left us something quite unique, something that is difficult to learn, or rather relearn – to stop our many tensions and interferences with our own innate good balance and coordination. I slowly adapted to living alone, running the training course and teaching private pupils. Without those commitments I could have gone to pieces – I derive energy from people and the Work.

My daughter, Lucia wrote this obituary about her father:

My parents Elisabeth and Dick Walker have been teaching and continuing to learn the Alexander Technique all my life and it is a credit to their skill as teachers that they were able to share their delight, interest and understanding of Alexander work with me.

Since his death in January, Dick's family and students miss him and yet he left us all with so much that we can remember and enjoy. As a teacher and as a parent Dick was consistently generous and gentle. He gave without conditions; learning with him did not mean that I had to have the same opinions, being loved by him did not mean that I had to fulfil his expectations. I feel very privileged to have had Dick for my father and to have lived my life until now supported by his unconditional love, acceptance and respect. Dick was respectful towards everyone of all ages and interests and was always prepared to learn from as well as to teach others.

Paul Wolf, a former student of ours, who trained from 1984 to 1987, wrote:

At the Engelberg Conference Dick Walker was spotted by many of us as he cycled his bike through the village and up the valley to where he was camping. He had always had a great love of mountains so it was fitting that he would be camping beside a vigorous alpine stream rather than staying in rooms at the centre of the conference. He always came across as a reserved person, avoiding the limelight. By the end of the Engelberg congress, however, Dick and Elisabeth Walker were receiving a great deal of unsolicited attention and were asked to join the panel of eminent teachers who took on the questions on the final morning.

Dick and Elisabeth taught pupils the Alexander Technique for over forty years before deciding to pass on their understanding of the work to a small group of students who enrolled on their first training course in 1984. Dick was a constant presence on the course, giving his students the fullest grounding that he could offer in the principles of the work. Dick was a gentle teacher. He drew out the very best from his trainees, who were inspired by his consistently quiet example. His profound commitment to the Alexander Technique meant that he was confident about communicating its underlying principles. His refusal to be directive meant that his trainees were given the necessary opportunity to explore their own resistances to change. He helped his trainees to recognise that this work is about an unrelenting search for self-improvement and to recognise that ego and power have little to offer us on the way. He was constantly mindful to give attention to the fundamental essence of the work, using his hands and words in a consistently non-doing manner.

Dick was a man of great intellect, sparked by openness and an inquiring mind. He was also deeply spiritual. His humility and respect for others meant that he never attempted to impose his ideas upon anyone.

He was much loved by those he worked with, and he remains a constant presence for many of us when we teach our own pupils.

I also quote several passages from Roz Lewis' obituary. (She trained at the Oxford Alexander Training Course from 1988 to 1990 and exchanged work regularly with Dick during the last year of his life):

When Dick Walker died with such dignity in January of this year, the Alexander world lost one of its most complex and well-loved characters. To everyone who knew him, the loss was great – I don't think many of us truly knew or comprehended how well-loved Dick was until we attended his memorial gathering in the Oxfordshire town of Benson. It was as if our collective love and respect for Dick only then became focused, as one person after another described another facet of Dick's personality, and we began to truly know him as the very special person that he was. I'm sure no one will forget that moving and uplifting tribute to someone they loved so dearly for a long time.

Dick began his association with the Alexander Technique in 1936, when he was given The Use of the Self *to read. In those days Dick was a passionate and successful golf amateur. He was living on a shoestring in Scotland, practising golf all day, slowly building up his reputation and game in order to turn professional. He had already won the Northern Open twice and been highly placed in the German Open when he read* The Use of the Self *and hit upon the idea that the Alexander Technique might enable him to hit golf balls better.*

He headed down to London and signed up for a course of lessons with Alexander. According to Dick he was a bad pupil – he persuaded Alexander to let him onto the training course, although Dick's main aim was still to perfect his golfing swing.

Dick's enduring love and successful partnership with his wife Elisabeth was one of the cornerstones of his life, and it is impossible to underestimate the mutual contribution they made to each other. Elisabeth's practical, earthy busyness was the perfect foil to Dick's dreamy, quiet philosophical approach to life – Dick would often say he didn't need a filofax as Elisabeth was his personal organiser! Their deep regard and respect for one another was apparent to everyone who knew them.

Dick was such a lovely person, so generous with his love for others. Towards the end of his life, his Alexander work was still solid – not particularly remarkable or flashy, just 100 per cent direction and inhibition. I think as students we tended to underestimate the value of his consistent and simple approach – all too often we were looking for the 'experience' of another visiting teacher's hands, or to hear another's new ideas about the Technique. His unassuming nature was thankfully overridden at the Alexander Conference in Engelberg last year, when at last he and Elisabeth were recognised as the Master Teachers they had always been. Even then Dick seemed rather bemused about all the fuss!

Dick's life work was teaching the Alexander Technique, even though he maintained many interests in a full and varied life. He so loved passing on his knowledge to prospective teachers – it really gave him an enormous sense of purpose. He may not have been the most famous Alexander teacher of his generation, but he was greatly respected and truly loved by an enormous number of people. His leaving has left a hole in many people's lives. His beautifully simple appreciation of, and above all, total belief in, the rightness and appropriateness of the Alexander Technique, will live on in all those who were fortunate enough to have worked with him.

Barcelona
Olympics: Richard
on Jacana
Top: Dressage
Arena
Left: Negotiating
the difficult water
feature

7 Away

In 1991 before Dick died, Richard discussed selling his horse Jacana and Dick said 'No, let's buy him' because he wanted Richard to take Jacana to the Olympics in Barcelona. Later that year Richard was offered a place in the team and he was emphatic that I must sign up with a package tour of owners and supporters going to the games. My reply was that I preferred to take myself and camp. I was delighted when Lucia offered to come with me in our small camper van. We took our time driving through France, staying with friends en route and finding more friends in Spain with space for the van. Each morning we drove to the stables leaving the van under trees beside the entrance and collected our owners' passes which allowed us to enjoy the same freedom and hospitality as the competitors. We could now go into the stables, some were under canvas (which must have been very hot) but thankfully Jacana was in a permanent box.

Richard said to me, 'Mum, I am glad you didn't join the organised group, their accommodation is a distance away and they may miss the vet's inspection.' We walked the course several times in spite of the heat and thought some of the jumps horrific. The whole dressage and cross-country sections of the three day event were on separate days, all too exciting. Richard and Jacana were going well, according to the commentator, past one very testing jump. Sadly at a water jump, Jacana refused, so Richard had no chance of gaining a gold medal. The show jumping on the last day was in the stadium in Barcelona and here Richard and Jacana were one of the few that had a clear round.

Lucia and I took the opportunity to explore Barcelona admiring Gaudi's architectural triumphs. We got lost in the city on our way home but a helpful taxi driver suggested we followed him as he led us to our homeward route. We had two nights in French camp sites on our way home. This was a really remarkable and worthwhile trip.

After Dick's death, the Alexander Technique helped me enormously to deal with my grief and live a reasonable life as a single woman. After closing the training course in December 2000, I was able to do more travelling and I have enjoyed teaching on many courses and on the various Congresses. Every teacher has their own way of practising Alexander's principles and I really respect this. It has been a joy to have Lucia to accompany me to Australia, Philadelphia, San Francisco, Basel, Denmark, Spain, Amsterdam, Paris, Washington, Los Angeles, Japan, Jerusalem, Freiburg

Barcelona Olympics: Richard and Jacana show-jumping

(Germany) and Italy, and on a number of visits to New York and Ireland. I am often asked what would Alexander think of what has happened to his precious 'Work'. I think he would be happy to see how it has spread all over the world. Probably we don't teach to his high standard but we are still trying to show our pupils how they can stop interfering with their innate balance and coordination.

Helped by his partner Gwen Harrigan, David Garlick and Doris Dietschy organised a very successful congress at the University of New South Wales in 1994. Marjory Barlow, Erika Whittaker and I gave what was called 'master classes'. I had not had much practice in teaching large groups and was initially very nervous. My first class was in a lecture room with steeply sloping rows of seats. I was at the bottom of these so that most of the audience could not see any demonstrations until I decided to climb on to the table and there I showed volunteers various movements, like squatting and coming forward from the hips. I enjoyed the teaching and soon overcame my shyness. After working in Australia with Bruce Fertman and Michael Frederick, Lucia and I were invited to teach at Philadelphia, San Francisco, Santa Barbara, New York and Sweet Briar.

View of Barrier Reef island in Australia where Elisabeth snorkelled

In Sydney there were many opportunities for working with other teachers which is always so interesting and educational. During our stay there, David and Gwen took us to many places of interest in and around Sydney including a visit to the remarkable Opera House. After the Congress Lucia and I flew up to Cairns from where we took a bus to Port Douglas and there had a delightful seaside holiday walking, swimming and snorkelling along the Barrier Reef.

In March 1995 Lucia and I taught for the first time at Bruce and Martha Fertman's course in Philadelphia. Bruce wanted me to teach what he called 'Alexander's procedures'. There we met a number of teachers who have become close friends. I was surprised there were no chairs in his teaching room. We managed to unearth some so I could teach 'hands on the back of a chair' as well as some standing and sitting, which hadn't been part of their usual training. There was, however, a 'horse' so we could work with someone sitting in a saddle. Much of the time we taught large groups in a church hall with Bruce, Martha and assistant teachers.

They both gave us some good times, including the Jewish Friday night traditional ceremonies and the visits to the special Morris Arboretum with its variety of interesting sculptures and an abundance of flowering trees and shrubs showering the ground with their many coloured petals and filling the breeze with a fragrance of Spring.

Morris Arboretum near Philadelphia

From Philadelphia we flew to Los Angeles where Michael Frederick met us and we stayed with him in Ojai. While Michael was working, Lucia and I took the opportunity to walk and enjoy the beautiful surroundings. There were oranges dropping from the trees, clashing colours of Mesembryanthemum spread along the paths and hanging climbers in full bloom. Humming birds hovered sipping nectar just outside our room. We walked in the grounds of Krishnamurti School surrounded by grassy areas and their pet animals. All was such a new and exciting experience.

From Ojai we drove on to San Francisco to teach a five-day master class with Marjory Barlow at Frank Ottiwell's training rooms. We stayed with Rome and Art Earle. I had met Rome in London when she was sixteen and having lessons with FM. She and Art treated us like long-lost friends. This event was repeated the following year when we gave another workshop with Marjory Barlow in San Francisco. We hired a car a week before the workshop and borrowed camping equipment from Rome and Art. We drove to Yosemite National Park having an incredible week climbing up to the tops of the dramatic waterfalls. We camped beneath the gigantic Sequoia trees that made us feel like ants in comparison. Our tent was pitched next to some enthusiastic rock climbers, weighed down by modern equipment (crash helmets, karabiners, endless ropes, harnesses and so

Elisabeth in Ojai

Climbing the falls at Yosemite

on) – so different from our climbing days when we had only a hemp rope round the waist, no harness and very few pitons. They were going to climb on the hazardous face of El Capitan.

Back with the Earles I developed a feverish cold but somehow managed to stay on deck during teaching sessions and recuperated in between. But at the end of the week, returning to the airport, I felt really sick so I lay on the floor in the departure lounge. I was immediately pounced on by an enthusiastic medic who noticed my low blood pressure and ordered an ambulance. In my opinion all I needed was a paracetamol, but that was overruled and I was taken off to hospital. I cannot express how much of an over-reaction I considered all that fuss to be. A nurse took my temperature which immediately went to normal after she'd given me a paracetamol equivalent, but the doctor was sure I was really ill and put me through all sorts of tests including a blood test. I was kept there all day and couldn't leave until I'd got a 'well-enough-to-fly' certificate. We then had to find a hotel for the night and returned to the airport in the morning where they said they had not got permission from British Airways in London for me to fly home. I had to use all my Alexander powers of inhibition not to scream, 'I want to go home.' The permit eventually arrived and thankfully brought this saga to an end.

—

For a number of years, Lucia and I, as visiting teachers, taught at the ACAT School in New York. The first of these visits took place in 1996 when we stayed for a few days in Barbara Kent's apartment overlooking Central Park. We later moved to the seventeenth floor apartment of our friend, Katherine Cohen, with whom we stayed many times and who organised workshops for us. In another year, I stayed with Michael Gelb in his apartment overlooking the river but, as he lived across town from ACAT he suggested that we go to Beret Arcaya. She was so delightfully hospitable and three times we stayed in her loft. Once when we were invited to run a course organised for us, we stayed in the house of Troup and Anne Matthews.

I have found New York to be the most interesting and friendliest city that I have ever visited and so many of my best friends come from there. At weekends and in spare time, we rode the New York subway, caught buses, or just walked. We visited a wonderful array of spectacular museums and galleries, including the Met and the Guggenheim. I remember once walking across Central Park to the Guggenheim, an inspiring build-

At Katherine Cohen's apartment   *Beret Arcaya in her loft*

At end of workshop at Matthews' house:
Lucia, Ann and Troup Matthews, their daughter and Elisabeth

ing, designed to be light and airy, where we enjoyed varied exhibitions of art and sculpture.

On one occasion, when leaving London, it had been almost too hot to bear but it was snowing when we reached New York. Then, with Lucia and a dancer friend, we visited Ellis Island and its museum depicting New

A view across Central Park

Lucia and Kirstie at Ellis Island

York's first settlers. We took the boat that passed the magnificent Statue of Liberty and enjoyed a tremendous day out.

In 1996, when Lucia was living in a friend's house in Potsdam where she was dancing with a group, I stayed with her for a few days and we spent time discovering many wonderful places. We took the tram to the Sans Soucie park with its various terraces, gardens and statues and the enormous staircase leading up to the Schloss Sans Soucie. We continued to walk to the vast Neues Palais before resting our legs to have our picnic lunch. Once refreshed we took a tree-lined walk past picturesque wooden houses in the Alexandruska settlement and onto the lake where Lucia often swam. There we saw the Schloss Cecilien, where the Potsdam peace conference was held in 1945. Beside the lake was the Marmour Palais, a neo-classical building adding variety to the architectural buildings in Potsdam.

The following day Lucia took me to the Dutch Quarter comprising of an attractive street of red brick gabled houses built by the Dutch in the eighteenth century. We then went on to meet her friends from the dance group who were living in a squat and then trying to keep out the cold. Later I was able to watch some of their dance before joining the group at their weekly party. There were a huge variety of appetizing home-cooked

Potsdam – Dutch Quarter

dishes provided by the participants. It was a wonderful finale to my visit to Potsdam.

I was collected from there by Vesna, a German friend who had been a pupil of mine in Oxford. She and her husband and two daughters had returned to Berlin because of his science work. They housed and fed me royally, and Vesna drove me round Berlin showing me so many beautiful buildings, the opera house and the new national gallery built mainly of glass and steel. At the Schoenberg town hall we climbed the 230 foot high tower to the Liberty bell which was a mountaineers' climb. We went on to the memorable Brandenberg Gate, a magnificent structure and then on to see the remains of the Wall and Checkpoint Charlie. I was interested in the new church that had been built beside the Emperor William Memorial Church which had been gutted by bombs during the Second World War and was reminiscent of our Coventry Cathedral which had also been gutted by bombs during that war. In fact both churches had exchanged symbols of peace. The remains of the old church were being used as a museum and on display was a cross of old nails retrieved from the charred rafters of Coventry Cathedral, a wonderful symbol of reconciliation following those horrific devastations in both countries. The new church was a hexagonal building with blue glass walls sending diagonal streams of coloured light, like faceted jewels, dancing on the altar and pews. This seemed to me the Germans' declaration of their move into a new era of peace.

On the last day Vesna took me to the Charlottenberg Palace, another elaborate palace with beautiful gardens. It had also been badly damaged by bombs during the wars and has been wonderfully repaired and is now a grand palace with grounds open to the public.

The Alexander Technique Congress in Jerusalem (1996) was another exciting event, this time organised by Shmuel and Ora Nelken and their team. Israelis have taken great interest in the Alexander Technique and there are some excellent teachers in Israel, many of them having been taught by Patrick Macdonald. Lucia was invited to give a master class there. Walter Carrington, Erika Whittaker and Marjory Barlow also gave master classes. As well as giving workshops we were able enjoy demonstrations and opportunities of sharing work with other teachers.

The congress was held in the university on Mt Scopus, overlooking the city and the hills beyond. From the roof we had views for miles around and our hosts organised tours to visit all the biblical sites: the Mount of

Olives, the Garden of Gethsemane, the Church of the Holy Sepulchre, the gold dome mosque, and the Dome of the Rock. This was a wonderful opportunity to visit the many places we had been told about from childhood and schooldays and religious studies. Being there passed all expectations. The Weeping Wall with the crowd of black-hatted, praying, bearded Jews is said to be the holiest place of prayer for members of the Jewish faith. Everywhere, there seemed to be respect for individual spiritual beliefs. The Church of the Nativity in Bethlehem, so important for Christians, was kept quiet and dimly lit for devotions. The city walls and gates were full of the atmosphere of bygone centuries. Whilst shopping in the Arab markets in the Old City, we were overcome by the colours, sounds and smells.

I have a lasting memory of the Yad Vashem memorial to the holocaust victims with its many moving pieces of sculpture and particularly the Children's Memorial, erected to the memory of 1.5 million children and babies killed in the death camps. Inside it was dark, except for hundreds of pinpoints of light, like stars representing the life of a child; it was so sensitive and evocative.

There were also visits to the Dead Sea and into the desert. One seemed to absorb the whole atmosphere of the Holy Land. I felt privileged to be

Lucia at the Yad Vashem memorial to the holocaust children

there, and go back in time to experience the history of this most important part of the world.

In 1997, I and friends Jean Lodge and Trish Baillie took my camper van on a holiday to Normandy and Brittany. My friends had a tent while I slept in the van. Jean and Trish had trained as Alexander teachers on my Oxford course. Jean is an artist and has a studio in Paris and had previously been Head of Print-making at Ruskin College and is now a Life Fellow of New College Oxford. She has generously given me, as birthday presents, many examples of her work which decorate the walls of my flat. Trish and I took the ferry to Caen where we picked up Jean. Being a Canadian, Trish wanted to see Juno Beach where her compatriots had landed on D-Day so we made a stop there. Later, we drove onto Arromanches where we played ball on the beach beside the remains of the D-Day pontoons. American-born Jean was interested in the American landings so we also visited Omaha beach and the American War Cemetery at Pointe du Hoc and were reminded again of the thousands of men who had lost their lives on that treacherous steep landing.

Jean and Trish at Quimperle

We went on to tour Brittany and found more delightful campsites. As we registered at one of these, we found the gardienne listening to the funeral of Princess Diana.

—

In the next few years, Michael Frederick arranged for Marjory and me to give workshops in Basel and Paris. In both cities I also taught on training courses. After the Basel workshop, one of the participants, Kevan Martin wrote these words.*

The master (mistress?) class given by Marjory Barlow and Elisabeth Walker in Basel was my first opportunity of seeing these two illustrious teachers, with their rich experiences of both FM and AR Alexander, actually teaching in the flesh. The five days was a fascinating experience and the interaction of these two doyenne with contemporary teachers and teacher-trainees drawn from Switzerland, Germany, France and Israel, produced many engaging moments. What was most significant for me, however, was the emphasis given by the master teachers to the fundamental principles deduced by FM.

Marjory Barlow kept reminding us of the importance of thinking. 'Less doing and more thinking' was her elegant summary. Indeed it was the ideas expressed in Constructive Conscious Control of the Individual *that originally drew her into the work. She quoted FM as saying: 'We've got to get to the point where the whole body is informed by thought.' One participant asked her where he could find the source of FM's statement that, 'You can do what I do if you do what I did.' She said she had heard it from FM himself, but that in the retelling the crucial ending was always left off: '…but none of you want anything mental!' Marjory Barlow told us how, from their first lesson, she demonstrated the importance of thinking to her pupils. After their first lesson, she gave her new pupils no homework, but asked them to think of what she'd said and to note that, 'you never say "no" throughout the day.' It is this training to say 'no', to 'not-do', to allow time for rational thought and conscious choice that was so emphasised by both FM and AR, according to Marjory Barlow. She identified it as the single crucial difference that raised the Alexander Technique (head, neck and trunk?) above what she called 'body work'. 'If you're banging your head against the wall there is only one cure.' Another of*

★ Five-day master-class Workshop by Kevan A. C. Martin – a neurophysiologist working in Zurich on human vision and perception. This workshop took place 24-28 April, 1997 in Basel, Switzerland. Organised by Michael Frederick and convened by Doris Dietschy.

Elisabeth with Kevan Martin in Zurich

the many gems that emerged in the course of the five days was Marjory Barlow's reflection that through the work came a 'total knowing you're not putting it wrong.'

Elisabeth Walker held energetic classes, assisted by her daughter Lucia. She emphasised particularly the importance of allowing the head to be free to lead the movement. In answer to a question about what was 'primary control' she explained, 'It is a natural part of our function,' and that, 'our interference with the function of the primary control is the cause of all our difficulties.' We were reminded of FM's encouragement: 'You are all quite perfect, except for what you are doing.' We cannot do forward and upward. But we can 'stop interference with forward and up' which would then free the head and enable a better functioning of the whole. 'Everything in the work is indirect. Specific remedies don't work.' Whenever members of the class concerned themselves with anatomical details of which muscle and which joint, Elisabeth Walker reminded us that, 'words sometimes get in the way' and that FM had said, 'You can't change any part without affecting the whole.' In one of the many anecdotes related over the course of the five days, we heard that the children at the school run by FM turned out to be particularly good observers of interference in their teachers: 'You pulled your head back,' they would criticise. We found no such opportunities!

In teaching, both Elisabeth Walker and Marjory Barlow were shining exam-ples. As they had observed with FM, they too approached each individual as an individual. For Elisabeth Walker there were 'no rules about how you go about teaching people.' This was particularly relevant to the repeated question from the class as to why FM had not written down verbatim his directions or orders for each activity. And in teaching she 'did not want to make people change too dramati-cally, because then they focused on the change rather than the whole pattern.' For Marjory Barlow, 'the whole art is to link up what you are thinking and what the pupil is thinking to an experience.' Patrick Macdonald's dictum, 'If it goes wrong, it's my fault not yours', was repeated several times by Marjory Barlow, but it did not always seem to evoke the desired inhibition in the pupils with whom she was working! 'Never work it out mechanically,' she admonished them. Both master teachers explained by example how their experience of the work was continu-ally expanding. Each day their explorations and experiments with the work could bring some new insight.

Both teachers talked about truth in teaching: 'This work is absolutely truthful,' said Marjory Barlow: 'If you think you're wrong, then do it and you will discover. We are afraid to be wrong, but by being wrong we know what to do. Accept that being wrong is your friend, not your enemy.' But remember, 'if you don't look after yourself first you can't help anyone else'. Elisabeth Walker's advice to us

Marjory Barlow with Elisabeth

was touching and simple: 'Collect the truth into yourselves. Don't try and be like anyone else, or like FM. Be yourself as a teacher.'

The principal difference between the students in the class and the two master teachers was quite apparent. Elisabeth Walker and Marjory Barlow exuded from every pore absolute confidence in the principles they had been taught by FM and AR. By contrast the questions raised by the class of contemporary teachers and students revealed a relative lack of confidence that expressed itself as a concern to acquire the techniques of teaching the Technique rather than to obtain a clearer understanding of the principles discovered by FM. Our master teachers brought us directly (or should that be indirectly?) back to the fundamental principles. Their mastery of the principles discovered by FM has enabled them literally to live the Alexander Technique for their entire adulthood. And together they have contributed more than 120 years to the teaching and training of countless pupils in the Technique. Their direct connection to the sources in Ashley Place makes them unique and it was a privilege for us to have enjoyed their care, attention and patient instruction over the five days.

At one point in the workshop, Marjory Barlow looked up from her pupil who was lying on the table and said, with her by now familiar smile, 'This work makes you happy.' The gales of laughter that regularly swept Elisabeth Walker's classes effectively made the same point. Even at the end of a demanding session, both master teachers continued to radiate us with the joy that the daily practice of FM's principles had brought to them. Truth, and joy too? They confirmed for us what they known for a lifetime. Here is something of immense value.

Irene Lukanow-Sutter also organised several workshops in Basel each year for me and Lucia. She and her husband were so caring and hospitable, taking us to operas when he was playing double-bass in the orchestra and taking us to dinner to meet their delightful sons. After the course Kevan Martin took us by train to Zurich, showing us highlights including the Chagall windows in the Fraumünster. After dinner in his flat, which was full of original paintings, we ran for the train back to Basel. This gave me heart palpitations for the next month.

Basel has remained a special venue for us. It was a small enough city to walk to the colourful market and visit the Cathedral or take a tram to the workshop. We could feel at home among the familiar parks and streets. During these years I was improving my teaching and learning more and more of different needs and applications.

Heraklia Guonaris invited Lucia and me to Aarhus, Denmark. Heraklia, having trained with the Carringtons, was happy to accept the traditional FM style of teaching. As well as teaching her students and colleagues, she showed us the beauties of the harbour and surrounding countryside.

Lucia and Doris Dietschy walking to the workshop at Basel

On two occasions we taught in Germany at schools run by Bruce Fert-man's assistants. This introduced us to different cities, people and teach-ers.

In Amsterdam there are two good Alexander training courses, and I have had the pleasure of teaching at both. Before my first visit to Paul Versteeg and Tessa Marwick's course they took me to see the sea and to a popular sandy beach for lunch, and also on a boat trip, round and through Amsterdam, seeing the houseboats and restaurants on the canals. Their spacious teaching room overlooked a canal, so there was never a dull moment between teaching sessions. On my next visit there, Penny Costley White came too and during free time we visited the Anne Frank house, which was a moving experience. The following day we spent time in the Rembrandt museum. We also taught at Arie Jan Hoorveg's course which was an educational experience, staying and teaching with this Dutch family, whose course included enthusiastic and dedicated students and teachers. We had an entertaining outing to the Van Gogh museum and our walks round and across the many canals encouraged us to return. For a passionate sightseer like me it was wonderful to have the opportunity during time off from teaching to explore all these interesting cities.

We flew out on Christmas Day 2001 to Michael Frederick's workshop in Santa Barbara, after which Lucia and I stayed with Lyn and Henry Charlsen who gave us a whirlwind introduction to exciting places nearby. Walking along Hollywood Boulevard we had a taste of show business. In contrast to the glamour of Hollywood they took us to see the Watts Towers, a group of 17 pieces of sculpture built by one man alone of scrap metal wire and broken china. One tower is 100 feet high. Another visit was to the amazing Getty Centre.

—

The next congress nearer home was in Freiburg, a delightful city in Germany where winters are mild and hibiscus survives outside through the winter. The streets and buildings are most attractive and streams flow beside the pavements with children paddling in them. Adorning these pavements are attractive mosaics. It was here that I saw for the second time a total eclipse of the sun.

We were so happy to be in Freiburg. Each congress has its own attractions and variety of events and opportunities of meeting like-minded people interested in the Alexander Technique. Each time, we seem to come away with new ideas and new friendships. A special evening was spent with Buzz and Pegs Gummeres sitting outside a restaurant watching the world go by.

Alexander Technique International (ATI) had several Annual General Meetings at Spanish Point in County Clare, Eire (2000, 2001, 2003 and 2007). I was invited as a guest and I was asked to demonstrate the way Alexander taught. I was enormously honoured to receive honorary membership of ATI with wonderful compliments. I met and made more new friends, many of whom had worked with Marjorie ('Marj') Barstow and it was interesting to notice their different ways of applying Alexander's principles. We were there by the sea in winter but Lucia swam with some other hardy souls.

—

In January 2001, having recently closed the Oxford training course, I was invited to New Zealand to Peter Grunwald's AT Natural Vision workshop, first at Mana in the Coromandel Peninsula and then in Auckland. I gave lessons to all the participants at Mana. I did enjoy the beautiful surroundings with views over islands in the Gulf and of blue, distant hills. Bush

Freiburg

Alexander Technique International

INCORPORATED

In Recognition and Appreciation Of

Elisabeth Walker

For her lifelong dedication to teaching and training and
for her remarkable outflow of energy and generosity of spirit
in sharing her wealth of knowledge and insight
to so many of us with such an open heart.
For this legacy, and for her friendship we are forever grateful.

Chair of ATI   November 13, 2000   Executive Secretary of ATI
        Date

walks and a visit to a beautifully laid-out water garden took place in free hours. We swam in a private pool surrounded by bush – still admiring the view. At Mana I was met by Louise Gauld who had invited me to stay in Auckland in a house beside a huge park in the centre of the city. My room looked out to One Tree Hill, one of Auckland's many small extinct volcanoes. Cattle and sheep (some black) often grazed there and I remember a huge bull eating bougainvillea over the fence. I was also entertained by 'the joggers and the doggers' passing by, undisturbed by the presence of bulls.

This trip to New Zealand was highlighted by the company of my friends Brigitte Cavadias and Marianne Moinot. They accompanied me to and from New Zealand. There they drove me south from Auckland to Wellington and Nelson. En route to Wellington we visited the Waitomo Caves where we floated in a boat watching glow-worms overhead. Since that trip, I have had wonderful holidays in Brigitte and Marianne's idyllic home in Provence.

After a night in Wellington with Juliet Shelley whom I had trained in Oxford, we took the ferry to the South Island and visited Marjory Fern in Nelson. From there I flew alone to stay in Christchurch with Sylvia Abercherle, a former pupil who had trained at our Oxford course, who entertained me royally.

Rabbit Beach, Nelson, New Zealand

In 2002 Lucia and I went to Japan and were met in Tokyo by Eriko Matsumoto who was shocked to see me arrive in a wheelchair as she had arranged many lessons for me to give. She was correspondingly relieved when I sprang out of it to greet her. We gave workshops in Tokyo before taking the train to the huge YMCA conference centre near Gotemba where Jeremy Chance organises large workshops every May during Golden Week. When I asked a student to what he would like to apply the AT, he said, 'Holding an umbrella.' From the venue there were wonderful views of Fujiama. Hatsuko Kayahara, a teacher who trained in Oxford, took us out one day. Later that day, my grandson William, who was teaching in Japan, arrived to join us for a weekend.

From there we went on to Kyoto where Jeremy took us to his home to meet his wife and new baby. With him we visited a beautiful temple. The last day in Kyoto we spent in the Botanic Gardens with Bruce Fertman and were fascinated with the many kindergarten children in all their different uniforms, all of them squatting to watch a performance there. That evening we taught at a training course organised by Bruce and run by Midori Shinkai.

Elisabeth's grandson, William with Mount Fuji

Sulphur fumes from Mount Kumiyama

The Oxford Congress in 2004 was considered to be special. It was one hundred years since FM had arrived in England. My daughter Lucia, Jean Fischer and Peter Ribeaux organised this in a remarkable way. Seven hundred or more participants had a great number of different workshops to choose from, as well as having interesting talks from people outside the Alexander community. Students could stay in a unique Oxford college or youth hostel. I had Meade Andrews and Ann Johnson staying with me. Visitors from home and abroad greatly enjoyed the architecture of the colleges. I gave my master classes in the Town Hall but I received most praise by cycling along the High Street.

For over twenty years, Michael Frederick and others have organised a two week workshop at Sweet Briar College in Virginia. We were asked to teach there in 2000 and are still making an annual visit. On the first three occasions, we flew into Washington D. C. and stayed with Meade Andrews for a few days. In our time with her, we were able to visit, among other places, the extremely interesting Gallery of Art and the Roosevelt Memorial. Meade arranged a workshop for us on the Saturday and drove us onto Sweet Briar on the Sunday. The first year, as the Dalai Lama was giving a talk, we delayed our journey in order to hear him. After Meade had moved, we continued making our own way to Sweet Briar.

Sweet Briar is one of my favourite teaching venues, though getting there in recent years takes some of the gilt off the gingerbread. Starting at home, deciding all the necessities to pack, mostly clothes for hot weather, and waterproofs and brolly and, of course, swimming togs and goggles and all the medications for internal and external use – including face creams, hand creams, sun tan lotion, mosquito repellent, after-bite cream, and it's all too much to remember.

I am collected from home at 6:50 am and taken to catch the 7:00 am bus to Heathrow Airport, where Lucia and I arrive at 9:00 am to check in for the 11:00 am flight to Washington D. C. Here we take a shuttle-bus to the car rental. At about 4:00 pm EST (five hours behind home time), Lucia drives expertly on towards Lynchburg, VA. It takes us about four hours, including the stops for the food for supper. At last, we reach Sweet Briar College. Oh, wonderful to be here again but, oh, how tired I feel. By the time I got to bed it would have been 1:00 am at home. Too long a day for me, but it has always been worth it.

We are a day early, so we go to the lake. On the way there we see a red flash and WOW, it is a bird, a cardinal. Then in front of the car there

Washington D. C.: Lucia with Meade beside river Potomac

are two white tails scurrying away, the tiniest bunnies almost complaining that we are invading their space. We stand on the jetty looking at the mirror-like surface of the water as a blanket of mist is just rising off it. At that moment the woodpeckers seem to be busy making more holes in a tree. In the water, which is warm and soft as silk, Lucia swims away towards the dam. In the water I luxuriate lying on my back watching the clouds. I turn over and see a figure peering through the mist. In the next moment it becomes a fisherman on a boat casting his line and the sun is on him. Looking further around I see two deer drinking, their golden brown images reflected in the glassy water. We all seem to be at peace and harmony in this idyllic spot. No wonder I enjoy this lake at Sweet Briar, especially at 7:00 am. The turtles, fish, beaver and many other wild creatures add to this nature wonderland.

The next day, nine other teachers arrive. They are all close friends and I have a special affection for each one. Our individual teachings of Alexander's principles may differ. This adds to our own learning process and creates a special harmonious environment for the students. The days here are arranged so all students have a great opportunity to experience the value of this variety of thought.

Students come from all walks of life with a wide range of experience. Many are from a performing arts background and are often very talented

Teachers at Sweet Briar

Two views of Sweet Briar

in their own art, whether it is music, dance or drama and it is a joy to witness these gifts at the end of each week in concert performance.

The two weeks here are such a highlight that saying goodbye is very difficult. The opportunity for Lucia and me to travel abroad together is one wonderful benefit that I have enjoyed since we closed the training course.

Sweet Briar: Dancing with one of the students

Two pictures that epitomise Sweet Briar
Above – The lake
Below – Elisabeth is presented with a 90th birthday cake

*Elisabeth and Dick
and their family*

*Left: Jo & Gavin, Dee and Mark with their
children,
Rebecca, William and Toya with Heidi
Middle: Richard and Louise
with their children, Jessica and Josh
Right: Sharyn and Lucia, Chris and Julia,
with their children, Quinn and Theo*

8 Family

Children have played a huge part in my life. Perhaps the devastating death of my eldest son made me value my sons and daughters even more. They have all been wonderful in their respective and different ways and have contributed so much and still do. My seven grandchildren and great-granddaughter are a great joy and they all teach me to stay in the present and to be 'cool'.

Gavin Russell – 5.8.1943

On returning from South Africa, Gavin trained as a chartered accountant.

Through an introduction by my brother Philip, in 1961, Gavin was articled to the firm of Barton Mayhew in the City of London. After qualifying in 1967, he continued to work for that firm until we moved to Oxfordshire when he got a job with a firm in Oxford. Since childhood in South Africa, where he sang in the church choir, he was strongly drawn to taking Holy Orders. In 1976, he gave up his high salary and trained at the College of the Resurrection in Mirfield, West Yorkshire, before being ordained in Wakefield Cathedral in 1978. After serving curacies in Wakefield and Northallerton, he became a vicar in the Church of England. Today, especially, this is a demanding profession. In 1979, he married Jo, a gifted and warm primary school teacher, who has been a great support. Gavin is still a huge help with family finances. He is now retired and has settled in Seascale, Cumbria. Following one of his visits to me, he wrote the following piece which has long been a great help to me:

When I sit with my mother – who am I?
Am I the child who misses my dead brother?
Or the one who perceives must replace him?
He was the eldest – my hero of five
My heart mourns him still fifty years on
He represents my doubts in living and dying
Full of life we played and explored imaginations
First born; he special and beloved by all
Year and a half superior – yet none of that remembered,
Only joy of acceptance perceived as filial love.
When called to part – he to paths glorious -
Ours to struggle on, alone and fearsome.

Could I become that which others had lost?
Could parents cope with grief of parting?
Neither had or received the comfort of the other.
Mother and child conceal their grief in pretence,
Acting out of fear of emotional weakness and tears.
Accountant, counsellor, priest, yet still child;
Sitting with mother enjoying her maternal love,
Acting out caring son, I am tax consultant still.
Business over, can I not attend her as friend?
Listening to her speak of matters that concern,
I hear not the octogenarian wisdom,
But the unintended criticism perceived by the child
Hides all wisdom as a 'sheep in Wolf's clothing'.
The child protests innocence, wisdom is shunned,
Discussion, gentle and loving, becomes remembered friction.
Are the hurts of the forefathers visited upon their children?
Or could it be that it is the other way round?
Our mutual concern is for the best in the other,
Matters concerning life now and in the hereafter,
Family members, their troubles, joys and strife,
If only all of us could hold on to the truth
That all will be well – a certainty absolute.
Alexander's Technique teaches 'forward and up':
Direction before moving – look before you leap.
God's spirit within enables our pilgrimage,
Walks beside us to encourage our endeavours.
Forward and up is Jacob's ladder for us all
Who desire of the best in ourselves and our neighbour.
This can only be possible when we truly perceive
The partnership of travellers on the journey of life:
Mutual help, encouragement, direction, laughter.
Participation is the principal in sharing.
Of all fellow beings, mother, your role is unique:
Playing your part in creation, you are concerned with my life.
You rejoice in my joys you hurt in my failures;
This role you share with Our Father in heaven
Who holds you and me in his wonderful arms,
Encourages our joy and heals our failings.
Darling mother, I hold you in so much regard;
As a child, I beg forgiveness for hurts of the past.

As adult, I know your love, in the image of the source,
Is interested, forgiving, enabling and loving.
You also need a healing and a comforting arm,
One who shares in those hurts and joys of your past.
Those who mothered you are in life eternal.
You are never outside the loving arms of the one
Who mothers and fathers, creates and gives life.
May you know his blessing now and always
And may those you mother be ever a joy.

Adrian Mark (now known as Mark) – 27.10.1947

From an early age, Mark was always pouring oil on troubled waters and out to help in any way. He went to the Ridge Preparatory school in South Africa and to Leighton Park, a Quaker school in Reading before going up to Cambridge University to read Natural Sciences. He then trained as a doctor at the Middlesex Hospital specialising in microbiology. He takes after my father in being very practical. He built his first house and is a great help to me when my plumbing goes wrong or when I need a new row of bookshelves. He and his wife Dee have three talented grown-up children: Rebecca, William and Victoria (Toya). Again like my father he has a passion for sailing. He built his first boat, a Cadet Class dinghy, which he launched at Dell Quay near Chichester for its maiden voyage. He has now bought a 38 foot Bermudan Sloop called *Freestyle*.

Richard Dorian – 16.8.1950

Dick and I knew nothing about horses though in South Africa a mulecart brought the milk. When Richard was a baby we were woken at 6:00 am by him calling 'gee-gee' at the sound of the milkcart. From then on his interest was anything on four legs but really ponies or horses. His special birthday present at the age of eight was a riding hat and being allowed to join a children's riding group trotting through the veld. Without instruction he took his mount happily and fearlessly over fences.

Back in England, besides riding on the Phillimores' horses, he was lent ponies to ride at gymkhanas and won cups for best rider and so on. We always wondered from where this special gift came. Marjorie Hance who trained the Cowdrey Pony Club taught him some dressage and he went on to win a major equestrian event at Burghley.

When we returned to England, Richard started at a prep school in London. However, when he became ill, we saw that, after the freedom of South Africa, he was too confined there and so he went to Highfield Prep

Richard, as a member of the Great Britain Eventing Team in 1969 at Haras du Pin

School in Hampshire, where he excelled at most sports. He went on to St Edward's School, Oxford, and then aged sixteen to Lars Sederholm for equestrian training.

As a family, we travelled abroad to watch Richard competing in international championships. In 1968 he won the junior European championships at Craon in France and in 1969 he was one of the winning British team in the European championships at Haras du Pin in France. We all travelled to these events and slept in our camper van. These were delightful and fascinating visits. That same year Richard won the Badminton International three-day event championship. He was eighteen and still remains the youngest winner. He and his wife Louise have two children, Jessica and Josh, and they run an equestrian training centre in Leicestershire.

Julia Josephine – 23.5.1953

From a young child Julia was always keen on clothes and of her own accord she would change into a prettier dress during the day. Her granny was horrified, saying, 'Children at home have to wear their dresses for a week.' At a very young age Julia was already using the electric sewing machine and making her own clothes. This interest in making clothes continued and she made her own beautiful wedding dress. She carried this interest on to knitting and opened a shop called Woolly Ideas. Julia always had a lot of blond curly hair and at two years old, with her curls coming down to the middle of her back, people would say: 'Oh, she is just like a little doll.' Richard got a bit jealous of this and one day, while playing with her, chopped off her hair at neck-length and hid the curls in the waste-paper basket, so that we wouldn't notice. Julia attended five different primary schools before going to Godolphin and Latymer Secondary School. From there she went on to the University of Sussex to read geography. It was during her schooling that she met her future husband Chris Cowper, a creative architect, and Julia has helped Chris in interior design. They have two boys, Quinn and Theo. Julia is now training to be an Alexander teacher.

Lucia Vivienne Diana – 25.2.1957

It was with great relief that by the time Lucia was born the approach to maternity care had changed and bed-rest was no longer considered essential. Lucia was born in a maternity home and I was allowed up and into the garden to be with the family soon after active birth. This became a good practice and the approach to childbirth was no longer treated as an illness.

When we first moved to England Lucia, aged four, went to ballet class, and she and another friend often had to demonstrate to the class. She continued ballet all through her schooling. Dance and movement have always been important to her. Lucia started at the junior part of Putney High School when she was four and stayed there until she took her GCEs, following which she moved to Oxford High School for her A levels. From there she went on to Cambridge to read anthropology. She started the performing dance group 'Joint Work' in Oxford and continuing from this interest she trained as an Alexander teacher and then taught on our training course, becoming a main assistant after Dick died. It has been so wonderful to have her to travel and teach with me all over the world. She and her partner Sharyn spend their holidays in Mozambique swimming out at sea with the dolphins.

After his ordination: Gavin with Dick

Mark's boat Freestyle *with his daughter Rebecca at the helm*

9 Reflections

Here are some of my reflections on a life-time's experience of the Alexander Technique, both as a student and as a teacher.

Pupils have different reasons for wanting lessons. Many come to improve their performance in some activity such as singing, dancing, acting or playing a musical instrument, even running or swimming. Others come with back or neck pain in spite of the fact that our work is primarily educational rather than therapeutic. Undoubtedly pains and aches often improve dramatically during the course of lessons.

With new pupils, I like to welcome them and ask how they have heard of the Technique and what in particular has interested them, and to find out their needs, their work and their daily activities. During the first lesson I do not spend time explaining how FM discovered his work but I do emphasise that it is a learning and thinking process and the importance of stopping bad habit patterns of functioning. This one does by inhibiting one's habitual responses to any stimuli. One is learning to take responsibility for one's own condition and to become more aware of the unnecessary tensions one makes in carrying out simple moves, thoughts and emotions. Many think the work is all about posture, but this is secondary to one's general improved use and coordination. Effective balance, poise and mechanism is the primary aim. FM often said, 'Use affects functioning'. He taught one to be in the 'present time'.

I find it difficult to teach the importance of 'thinking' as opposed to 'doing'. This thinking of directions is quite foreign to pupils. Teaching balanced coordination and the use of the limbs is of vital importance. Most of our early life we've been taught to make an effort – to try hard – often putting in lots of unnecessary tension. This can unbalance the whole coordination.

A lot of people say that FM didn't teach application work. He was teaching us to apply his principles to life, to everything we do. In early lessons he considered it important to use chair work because it is an activity we repeat many times a day and he had seen people misusing themselves so badly, pulling their heads back and shortening throughout, when moving to sit or stand. He taught the importance of stopping and inhibiting one's habitual way of performing any activity so, in private lessons, he chose to teach mostly sitting and standing. He said, if you can learn to inhibit your habitual way of carrying out this movement you are already improving your use.

I think it is very important at any stage to find out where one's pupil is coming from at that particular time. I nearly always ask them what their day-to-day activity is or was before they came for a lesson because it gives you some thought of what they have to deal with.

I emphasise again the importance of improving one's psycho-physical awareness including awareness of all around one, with special use of the eyes and engaging their panoramic vision, awareness of where one is, where one's feet are, where one's head is and whether one is cold or hot – all these sensitivities have a part to play in balance and coordination.

It is so important for pupils to remember that the individual is a coordinated whole and that any one part (especially the thinking) affects the entire being. One must remember to stop momentarily, and in the moment of stopping give oneself the opportunity to choose how to proceed.

The teacher must be thinking and directing as he/she puts hands on, noticing the pupils' condition, their use, their breathing, whether they are free and going up, and at the same time ensuring that they have a new experience. It is important that the teacher pays special attention to his/her hands when taking them off.

During a turn, sitting well back on the chair FM would put his velvet-covered cigar box between one's shoulder blades and the chair-back, allowing one to appreciate the directions in the back. I find it useful in a car, say, to arrange the back of the seat to be upright; this reminds me of the anti-gravity mechanism in my back.

Many pupils are interested in Alexander work to improve their 'posture' and some talk about having a straight back as though this is what we're teaching. We are in fact teaching more freedom, not less – and improved posture is an incidental result of stopping our interference with our innate balance.

Teaching people to think, inhibit and direct in early lessons is difficult because we have all been trained to try hard to get things 'right'. Many parents and teachers have said: 'Sit up straight', 'Pull your shoulders back', or even 'Drop the shoulders' and in doing so have demonstrated that they have no understanding of the importance of Alexander's teaching. These commands lead to unsatisfactory habit patterns, interfering with the whole coordination. The shoulders, arms and hands have become a particular interest of mine. An important direction is for the shoulders to be directed one away from the other allowing the wide shoulder girdle which permits plenty of life energy to remain in the arms. These ideas

Teaching: hands on back of chair

are particularly important when working with musicians. Another useful direction is up the sides and into the armpit as well as up the back and front as this helps to avoid the heaviness in the shoulders. The fingers and hands also want to be lengthening, with a free wrist and the direction going from the wrist to the elbow and from the shoulder to the elbow, with the energy coming from the whole being.

The use of the heel of the hand is often neglected even though it can give such excellent direction. A lengthened hand on the mid-back with the other on the diaphragm area and the teacher directing up, will allow the pupil to go up. The feet want to be lengthening and making good contact with the floor, but it is important to free the ankles, allowing the anti-gravity mechanism in the back to take one up out of the knees and hips.

The harmonious communication between the student and teacher as they go up together is the ideal experience for them both. The following quotation expresses well a good lesson.

The nature of an Alexander lesson is that of a mutual exchange between two beings, teacher and student. When all is working well it seems that there is neither leader nor follower but some magic carpet of energy that sweeps both participants in a shared common movement. Of course there is a unique skill that makes this possible, a skill that must be learned, it requires the recognition of a special quality of internal activity and the ability to call up that quality at will. In a sense what we teach in the course of a lesson is the susceptibility for this quality to be called up in the student (the only difference between teacher and student is that the teacher is hopefully more conversant with this quality, but this difference is indeed a very great one). *

A useful teaching aid is a 'saddle horse'. Sitting on this helps the pupil to send the sitting bones down, allowing the back to lengthen and widen (while maintaining head directions) and allowing the legs to lengthen out of the hip joints towards the floor. Pupils have often found that they have gained a new experience from sitting on the saddle with their thighs directing down out of the hips. A gentle, directed hand on the pupil's ankle helps them to lengthen through their whole being.

The Technique is really helpful in childbirth. I gave birth to two of my children on Irene Tasker's teaching table. I was kept in bed for two weeks following the birth of some of my children. Now one is encouraged to be active during delivery, crawling, squatting and some like water births and, unlike the birth of my first babies, new mothers are not kept in bed. I recommend plenty of ante-natal preparation in saying whispered 'ahs', squatting and crawling, and giving one's directions. Saying three whispered 'ahs' usually lasts through one contraction and helps the mother's breathing as well as giving her something useful to focus on instead of getting over-tense and over anxious. It also frequently relieves the pain. It helps the whole organism, including the baby.

FM in his early lessons in 1904 was known as the breathing man and this was how he first became recognised. Many interfere with their breathing, and singers and voice teachers often encourage a lot of tension in their form of teaching. As an Alexander teacher I notice that pupils and students do not enjoy saying whispered 'ahs'. They find the process unusual and they put in tensions. FM taught it to be enjoyable, to go through one's directions allowing the neck to be free, the back to lengthen and widen and to go up and think of something funny, to smile allowing the jaw to drop forward and the tongue to the top of the lower teeth letting the

---

*   Alex Farkas, writing in the *Alexander Journal* no. 21, 2006.

Whispered 'ah'   *Teaching lunge*

air flow out on the whisper 'ah' and then closing the mouth allowing the air to flow in through the nose. During the whole process the rib cage will contract and expand during exhalation and inhalation, and one should notice the throat being open and round and the sound made should give some indication of any excess tension, or doing. One should emphasise to one's pupils not to take a breath before starting a whispered 'ah' but to allow the first 'ah' to be shorter. Subsequent 'ahs' may be longer according to inflow of breath and the flexibility of the pupil's ribcage. I encourage pupils to say whispered 'ahs' during the day, in as many situations as possible (during a nice walk, while waiting in a queue). This can help one to become familiar with the process and to be able to say them without interference.

Coming forward from the hips is an important movement in daily activities. In applying FM's teaching, some teachers come forward from the hips before allowing the knees to bend. I more often suggest hingeing at the knees, then hingeing at the hips, remembering the fundamental head–neck–back relationship. Alexander's teaching does not stop you from doing what you want to do, but lets you apply the principles to activities, which is possible if you are not stuck with difficult habit patterns.

FM also showed us how from standing he could, leading with the head, roll forward to put his hands on the floor without bending the knees. It is important to remember that in reversing the procedure, one unfolds leading with the eyes, without tightening the neck.

Often FM would put his lengthened fingers on to the lower ribcage, noticing one's breathing and whether one was fixing or lifting there. Sometimes he used a hand on the top of the head noticing the lengthening throughout. This needs an experienced hand.

Having been a collapser myself, I still think it is difficult to teach a collapser. A collapser is nearly always pulling down in front, with over-stretched muscles in the back which are not giving support. You have to sort out so much and re-educate what is holding and what is allowing one's anti-gravity mechanism to come into play. You have to come back to thinking and directing. Think: 'That's my head and I'm not going to tighten under the chin or at the back of the neck.' Just allow the head to balance on the atlanto-occipital joint and from that joint you can let it nod forward and back and turn. Take advantage of any support available to you, to remind you of the anti-gravity mechanism of the back: in a car adjust the seat, in a chair use cushions as support to make yourself aware

Elisabeth teaching at the Sydney Congress

of your balance over the sitting bones. An opposite extreme is the over-fixed pupil who needs to be taught to free the neck, the hips, knees and the ankles. When we are tired, we often slump; instead, if possible, we should lie semi-supine on the floor or table, with a small support under the head. One can now continue directing the neck to be free and the back to spread out on the floor or table and the feet lengthening and the knees going up towards the ceiling. One wants to continue giving directions in this position to be of value to the whole.

There is a general misconception that FM was against exercise. In fact he was only against remedial exercises. When they encouraged even more

Going onto toes

misuse, he saw that the individual was often taught to put a lot of extra tension and shortening throughout when gaining the required end. Of course he liked to help people take exercise applying the Technique; an example of this occurred when he helped Dick to improve his golf. He liked to teach people to attend to their own use while exercising. He himself rode horses and walked a lot. He had a light step, allowing the ground to send him up, his head leading. Some of the exercises in the gyms today are done with too much effort to be beneficial to the whole. Pilates, Tai Chi and yoga can be good when applying AT directions. Alexander Technique is basic and fundamental to all activities, including life itself. It requires one to think and stop one's habitual responses and to allow one's innate good directions to come into play – all quite subtle, but practical.

FM did a lot of application work and pointed it out. That's why he did whispered 'ahs' – because you're always speaking and breathing – also

Elisabeth cycling to Oxford Congress

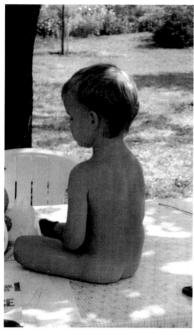

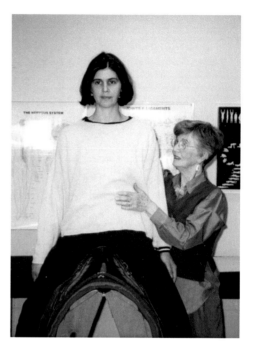

Picture used by Elisabeth to show how
a youngster may sit naturally

Teaching on a saddle

'hands on the back of the chair' to teach a pupil how to apply his principles to an unusual activity. When he first came to this country he went to different theatres to teach actors and actresses, applying his work to help them speak and move. FM used to stand in the wings at the theatre and observe and teach from there. I have a printed testimonial that lists the actors who wrote to him to say 'thank you', including Henry Irving.

It is important to relate the Technique to the individual's needs. Sitting, standing, walking, writing, answering the phone, carrying an umbrella; all these things involve application work. I once taught a writer who was having a lot of trouble with her writing arm so we sat at the table and did some writing.

It is difficult in the early stages to teach one's pupil to stop trying to make the changes, but to allow the teacher to help them to think and direct.

Our children disliked being asked what their parents did; we suggested they reply, 'They teach psycho-physical re-education'. No one knew what that meant so the question was usually dropped, though later they might have said, 'They teach them to inhibit one's habitual response to a stimu-

Pictures used by Elisabeth when teaching to portray freedom of movement

One of Elisabeth's aunts ca. 1900

A child in South Africa enjoying the beach

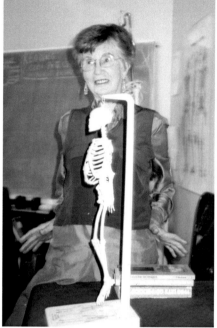

A flautist on the saddle   *Teaching with the skeleton*

lus.' I personally don't think the Alexander Technique can be put into words, one needs the experience that can be made with the help of the teacher. Changes are so subtle and take their time to become conscious. New pupils and students often evaluate their teacher: as their psycho-physical state improves, their evaluation might change. Changing teachers can help them reassess by listening afresh to the guidance of their previous teacher. I believe empathy is important between student and teacher.

It takes time to re-educate sensory awareness, and feelings are unreliable (FM talked of 'debauched kinaesthesia'). This awareness seems to vary in individuals. There seems to be no consistency in how a pupil becomes aware of the changes brought about by the Technique. Some notice their improved use in the early stages and some take years to notice the change (though often their friends and family have been aware of this improvement as it occurred).

During my years teaching at Sweet Briar in America, I have worked with many teachers who were taught by Marj Barstow who trained on FM's first training course, qualifying in 1934. They learned a lot about group teaching through her. Working with groups is particularly helpful in improving general and specific awareness. By general awareness, I mean being totally aware of one's environment, the floor, the sky, the room, members of the group. Specific awareness is being aware of one's own thinking and moving in relation to one's own freedom.

It's most encouraging as a teacher to notice with one's hands that the psycho-physical memory of previous lessons has been retained. For example, my experience is that a pupil who has had a gap of twenty-five years has still retained a large amount of good balance and coordination as a result of those early lessons.

I am often asked by parents to give their child a lesson because of their bad posture. I prefer to take children because they have some interest in the value of applying Alexander's ideas, such as young musicians or children interested in sport, because they can notice how it improves their performance in an applied activity. This helps to retain their interest.

My own satisfying experience was with a five-year old considered to be backward. Although she was very gentle, she was a slow learner, her coordination was poor, and she dribbled. She was happy to come and seemed to enjoy the extra attention and made such good progress in her lessons that her doctor suggested that she should continue. She improved so much that she was sent to school with her sisters, but sadly the parents did not see the importance of continuing the lessons once she was able to start 'normal' school.

It would be wonderful to teach teenagers because of their growth spurts and hormonal changes for I believe that at this stage they are laying down the foundations of future growth and use. However they are probably the most difficult to teach because they like to collapse and pull down like their friends.

Musicians have said to me that they cannot give their directions while playing. I say to them: 'Think of it when you're not playing, for better use carries you through.' We are re-educating the nervous system and the more often we can think of giving our directions the more we improve our use. Our re-educated condition becomes a part of our being and carries us through the times when our attention is elsewhere.

The important principles are: allowing the neck to be free, the back to lengthen and widen and to gradually become more balanced and coordinated. That's why the teacher has to put a lot of attention on his or her own use, to hand on these thoughts and thinking abilities to his or her pupils, at whatever stage.

Use what works for you. What works for me, for instance, when I'm bouncing on my little trampoline at home, is thinking of the heels going down and my neck being free. I don't think specifically of collarbone or creating new neural pathways. That whole psycho-physical awareness is what we need.

I recommend having lessons from different teachers. Do not think that any one teacher has all the answers for you. Find out what you can learn for yourself from different teachers and what makes sense to you. And rethink if there's a better idea or a different idea that can help you.

The following are some of FM's favourite aphorisms I quote when teaching:

Of course you must remember your directions to project them. But you're not satisfied with that; you will try to feel out whether the thing is working out right or not.

Like a good fellow, stop the things that are wrong first.

Don't you see that if you 'get' perfection today, you will be farther away from perfection than you have ever been.

In writing my memoirs, I'm remembering the enormous changes that have taken place in the world in the last ninety-three years. We all adapt to and hopefully appreciate the many discoveries and improvements. Despite two horrific world wars and conflict in other countries and mistakes such as DDT sprays and global warming, on balance scientific discoveries, especially medical, have advanced us to a remarkable wealth of knowledge. For me, radio and television give a lot of pleasure and help me to keep in touch with what's going on in the world. My favourite viewing on the television is wildlife programmes and sport.

In my nineties now, I have moved to a flat, convenient but not beautiful. Sometimes it is sad to be just me – no husband, no children, and no dogs (demanding walk or food), no river or sea to enjoy – but out of my window, I can see very small children in the playground below, tinies daring to use the slide, then dashing to the see-saw, wanting something different. With amusement, I notice the children full of life and well-coordinated while often the parents and carers sit on a bench, looking bored. While on the phone, I look out of another window, watching the birds and on a small patch of water, a duck and drake flirting, it's mating time, but a moorhen comes and disturbs all, as this is her patch, and she drives them away. No longer am I able to admire the colourful drake, watching time is over, I have pupils to teach: preparing to give some lessons in the Alexander Technique, thinking of the needs and interests of each individual and how I can help them to think and stop 'doing' the things that are interfering with their balance and coordination.

Teaching has been a most extraordinarily rewarding experience. Communication by touch is probably the most basic form of communication. And what is one communicating? The answer very simply is 'life'. This sounds a rather grand claim, but every teacher will bear me out. The pupil becomes more 'alive' no matter whether he is stuck in a state of collapse or stuck in a condition of over-tension. But whether the pupil is aware of this greater aliveness or not, the teacher is, and this is what is most rewarding. Because one knows with absolute certainty that what one is communicating is good.

Index of Names

Page numbers in italics refer to pictures.